Sweet Shoes for Wee Ones

Designs by Kristi Simpson

We're serving up the sweetest collection of shoes, boots, sandals and loafers for Baby in this collection of footwear from designer Kristi Simpson. With 15 designs, there's at least one on the menu that is just right for every occasion. Be prepared for multiple requests for this adorable footwear!

Table of Contents

Fun in the Sun

Skill Level
 ■■□□ EASY

Finished Sizes
Instructions given fit size small; changes for medium and large are in [ ].

Finished Measurements
2½ inches wide x 3½ inches long *(small)* [2½ inches wide x 4 inches long *(medium)*, 2½ inches wide x 4½ inches long *(large)*]

Materials

4 MEDIUM

- Medium (worsted) weight cotton yarn:
  2 oz/100 yds/56g each hot pink and turquoise
- Size F/5/3.75mm crochet hook or size needed to obtain gauge
- Yarn needle
- 4 stitch markers

Gauge
4 sc = 1 inch; 4 sc rnds = 1 inch

Pattern Notes
Weave in loose ends as work progresses.

Join with slip stitch as indicated unless otherwise stated.

Chain-3 at beginning of row counts as first double crochet unless otherwise stated.

Chain-2 at beginning of row counts as first half double crochet unless otherwise stated.

Special Stitches
Beginning crocodile stitch (beg crocodile st):
Ch 3 *(see Pattern Notes)*, 4 dc down post of first dc of previous rnd, ch 1, 5 dc up next dc post.

Crocodile stitch (crocodile st): 5 dc down next dc post, ch 1, 5 dc up next dc post.

Sandals

Sole
Make 2 each hot pink & turquoise.

Rnd 1: Ch 11 [13, 15], sc in 2nd ch from hook, sc in each of next 3 chs, hdc in each of next 3 [4, 5] chs, dc in each of next 2 [3, 3] chs, 6 dc in last ch, working on opposite side of foundation ch, dc in each of next 2 [3, 3] chs, hdc in each of next 3 [4, 5] chs, sc in each of next 4 chs, **join** *(see Pattern Notes)* in beg sc. *(24 [28, 32] sts)*

Note: *For left Sole, attach stitch marker on 2nd dc of 6-dc group of rnd 1. For right Sole, attach stitch marker on 5th dc of 6-dc group of rnd 1.*

Rnd 2: Ch 1, 2 sc in same st as beg ch-1, sc in each of next 3 [3, 4] sts, hdc in each of next 3 [4, 5] sts, dc in each of next 2 [3, 3] sts, 2 dc in each of next 6 sts, dc in each of next 2 [3, 3] sts, hdc in each of next 3 [4, 5] sts, sc in each of next 3 [3, 4] sts, 2 sc in last st, join in beg sc. *(32 [36, 40] sts)*

Rnd 3: Ch 1, sc in same st as beg ch-1, 2 sc in next st, sc in each of next 2 [3, 3] sts, hdc in each of next 6 [7, 9] sts, [hdc in next st, 2 hdc in next st] 6 times, hdc in each of next 6 [7, 9] sts, sc in each of next 2 [3, 3] sts, 2 sc in next st, sc in last st, join in beg sc. *(40 [44, 48] sts)*

Rnd 4: Ch 1, sc in each of next 2 sts, 2 sc in next st, sc in each of next 2 [3, 3] sts, hdc in each of next 6 [7, 9] sts, [hdc in each of next 2 sts, 2 hdc in next st] 6 times, hdc in each of next 6 [7, 9] sts, sc in each of next 2 [3, 3] sts, 2 sc in next st, sc in each of next 2 sts, join in beg sc. Fasten off. *(48 [52, 56] sts)*

Assembly

Holding 1 Sole each color tog, with turquoise on top, thread yarn needle with a length of hot pink and, working through both thicknesses, sew tog with **running stitch** *(see illustration)* through sts of rnd 4.

Running Stitch

Top
Make 2.

Row 1: With hot pink, form a **slip knot** *(see illustration)*, pull yarn through marked st, ch 3 *(this will be between toes)*, holding finger on next ch, ch 6, dc in ch that is being held *(first of the ch-6)*, this will now be a triangle, **beg crocodile st** *(see Special Stitches)*, using the ch as a post work **crocodile st** *(see Special Stitches)*.

Row 2: Working back across row, **do not turn**, ch 3, dc in same st, 2 dc in center of crocodile st, 2 dc in end of crocodile st *(this will be the previous ch-3 from row 1)*.

Row 3: Beg crocodile st, sk next 2 dc, crocodile st. *(2 crocodile sts)*

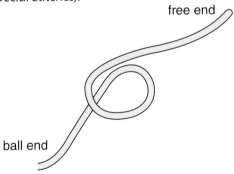

Slip Knot #1

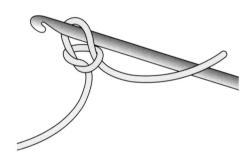

Slip Knot #3

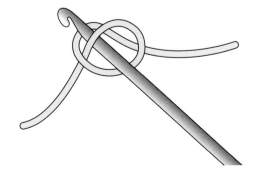

Slip Knot #2

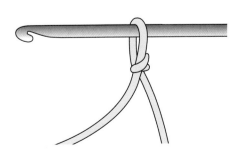

Slip Knot #4

Row 4: Working back across the row, **do not turn**, ch 3, dc in same st, 2 dc in center of crocodile st, 2 dc in center of 2 dc from row 2, 2 dc in center of next crocodile st, 2 dc in end of crocodile st.

Row 5: Beg crocodile st, [sk next 2 dc, work crocodile st] across.

Strap

Row 6: Ch 1, sl st in center of last crocodile st, ch 14 [16, 18], using care not to twist the ch, sl st in center of the crocodile st on opposite side, turn.

Row 7: Ch 2 *(see Pattern Notes)*, hdc in each ch across, sl st in center of crocodile st. Fasten off.

Assembly

With yarn needle and length of hot pink, sew side corner of each outer edge crocodile st to edge of Sole. Fasten off. ●

Modern Jane

Skill Level

 EASY

Finished Sizes

Instructions given fit size small; changes for medium and large are in [ ].

Finished Measurements

2 inches wide x 3 inches long *(small)* [2 inches wide x 3½ inches long *(medium)*, 2 inches wide x 4 inches long *(large)*]

Materials
- Medium (worsted) weight acrylic yarn:
  2 oz/100 yds/56g brown
  1 oz/50 yds/28g teal
- Size D/3/3.25mm crochet hook or size needed to obtain gauge
- Tapestry needle
- Sewing needle and thread
- 10mm buttons: 4
- Stitch markers: 4

4 MEDIUM

Gauge

5 sts = 1 inch

Pattern Notes

Weave in loose ends as work progresses.

Join with slip stitch as indicated unless otherwise stated.

Chain-2 at beginning of round **does not** count as first double crochet unless otherwise stated.

Shoe
Make 2.

Rnd 1 (RS): With brown, ch 10 [12, 15], sc in 2nd ch from hook, sc in each of next 3 [4, 5] chs, sl st in each of next 1 [2, 2] ch(s), sc in each of next 3 [3, 5] chs, 6 hdc in last st, working on opposite side of foundation ch, sc in each of next 3 [3, 5] chs, sl st in each of next 1 [2, 2] ch(s), sc in each of next 4 [5, 6] chs, **join** *(see Pattern Notes)* in beg sc. *(22 [26, 32] sts)*

Rnd 2: Ch 1, 2 sc in first st, sc in each of next 6 [8, 11] sts, hdc in next st, 2 dc in each of next 6 sts, hdc in next st, sc in each of next 6 [9, 12] sts, 2 [0, 0] sc in last st, join in beg sc. *(30 [33, 39] sts)*

Rnd 3: Ch 1, 2 sc in first st, hdc in each of next 8 [10, 13] sts, [sc in next st, 2 sc in next st] 6 times, hdc in each of next 8 [10, 12] sts, 2 sc in next st, draw up a lp of teal, join in beg sc. *(38 [40, 47] sts)*

Rnd 4: Ch 2 *(see Pattern Notes)*, dc in each st around, join in first dc. *(38 [40, 47] sts)*

Rnd 5: Ch 1, sc in each of next 7 [8, 10] sts, **sc dec** *(see Stitch Guide)* in next 2 sts, sc in each of next 2 [2, 4] sts, sc dec in next 2 sts, [sc in next st, sc dec in next 2 sts] 5 times, sc in each of next 2 [2, 4] sts, sc dec in next 2 sts, sc in each of next 6 [7, 8] sts, draw up a lp of teal, join in beg sc. Fasten off brown. *(30 [32, 39] sts)*

Rnd 6: Ch 2, dc in each of next 9 sts, [**dc dec** *(see Stitch Guide)* in next 2 sts] 6 times, dc in each of next 9 sts, join in first dc. *(24 [26, 33] sts)*

Rnd 7: Ch 1, sc in each of next 3 [5, 5] sts, sl st in each of next 5 [5, 8] sts, [sc dec in next 2 sts] twice, sc in next st, [sc dec in next 2 sts] twice, sl st in each of next 5 [5, 8] sts, sc in each of next 2 [2, 3] sts, join in beg sc. *(20 [22, 29] sts)*

Straps

Note: *Find center back, place stitch marker in 4th st from each side of center (8 [8, 10] center sts on back of heel).*

Row 1: With teal, ch 14 [15, 17], sl st in each of 8 [8, 10] center sts on back of heel, ch 16 [17, 19], turn.

Row 2: Dc in 4th ch from hook, dc in each ch, dc in each of next 8 [8, 10] sts, dc in each ch across. Fasten off.

Sew 1 button to each side of row 2 of Shoe. Using natural sps at end of each Strap for buttonholes, cross Straps and button. ●

Cupcake Cutie

Skill Level
 **EASY**

Finished Sizes
Instructions given fit size small; changes for medium and large are in [ ].

Finished Measurements
2 inches wide x 3 inches long *(small)* [2 inches wide x 3½ inches long *(medium)*, 2 inches wide x 4 inches long *(large)*]

Materials

- Medium (worsted) weight acrylic yarn:
    2 oz/100 yds/56g each cream and pink
- Size D/3/3.25mm crochet hook or size needed to obtain gauge
- Tapestry needle
- Sewing needle
- Sewing thread
- 12mm buttons: 2
- Stitch markers: 4

Gauge
5 sc rnds = 1 inch; 6 sc sts = 1 inch

Pattern Notes
Weave in loose ends as work progresses.

Join with slip stitch as indicated unless otherwise stated.

Chain-2 at beginning of row **does not** count as a half double crochet unless otherwise stated.

Special Stitch
Surface slip stitch (surface sl st): Insert hook RS to WS, holding yarn on WS, draw up a lp and draw through to RS, insert hook in next st, yo, draw up a lp and draw through st on hook.

Sandals

Sole
Make 2 each pink & cream.

Rnd 1 (RS): Ch 8 [10, 12], 2 sc in 2nd ch from hook, sc in each of next 5 [7, 9] chs, 4 sc in last ch, working on opposite side of foundation ch, sc in each of next 5 [7, 9] chs, 2 sc in last ch, **join** *(see Pattern Notes)* in beg sc. *(18 [22, 26] sc)*

Rnd 2: Ch 1, 2 sc in first st, sc in each of next 6 [8, 10] sts, 2 dc in each of next 4 sts, sc in each of next 6 [8, 10] sts, 2 sc in last st, join in beg sc. *(24 [28, 32] sts)*

Rnd 3: Ch 1, sc in first st, 2 sc in next st, sc in each of next 5 [7, 9] sts, hdc in next st, [dc in next st, 2 dc in next st] 4 times, hdc in next st, sc in each of next 5 [7, 9] sts, 2 sc in next st, sc in last st, join in beg sc. *(30 [34, 38] sts)*

Rnd 4: Ch 1, sc in first st, 2 sc in next st, sc in next st, 2 sc in next st, sc in each of next 5 [7, 9] sts, [sc in next each of next 2 sts, 2 sc in next st] 4 times, place stitch marker in first sc of next sc group, sc in each of next 5 [7, 9] sts, [2 sc in next st, sc in next st] twice, join in beg sc. Fasten off. *(38 [42, 46] sts)*

Assembly
With WS of 1 each pink and cream Soles tog, with cream, facing and working through both thicknesses with pink, **surface sl st** *(see Special Stitch)* in each st around, join in beg sl st. Fasten off. Join rem 2 Soles in same manner.

Toe
Make 2.

Row 1: Join pink at stitch marker placed on rnd 4 of Sole, **ch 2** *(see Pattern Notes)*, hdc in same st as beg ch-2, **hdc dec** *(see Stitch Guide)* in next st, [hdc in next st, hdc dec in next 2 sts] 5 times, turn. *(12 sts)*

Row 2: [Hdc dec in next 2 sts] 6 times, turn. *(6 hdc)*

Row 3: [Hdc dec in next 2 sts] 3 times, turn. *(3 sts)*

Rows 4–13 [4–15, 4–15]: Ch 1, sc in each of next 3 sts, turn. At the end of last rep, leaving a 10-inch length, fasten off.

To create a lp, fold row 13 [15, 15] under and sew to row 8 [10, 10].

Heel
Note: *Find center back st, count 6 sts to each side and mark with stitch marker.*

Left Sandal
Row 1: Join pink at right stitch marker, ch 1, sc in each of next 11 sts, turn.

Row 2: Ch 1, sc in each st across, turn.

Row 3: Rep row 2.

Row 4: Ch 1, sc in each st across, ch 18 [20, 20], turn.

Row 5: Sc in 5th ch from hook *(button lp)*, sc in each rem ch, sc in each sc across Heel. Fasten off.

Right Sandal
Row 1: Join pink at left stitch marker, ch 1, sc in each of next 11 sts, turn.

Rows 2–5: Rep rows 2–5 of Left Sandal.

Flower
Make 2.

Row 1: With cream, ch 31, sc in 2nd ch from hook, [sc in next ch, dc in next ch] across, leaving a 12-inch length, fasten off.

Starting at center, roll row 1 to form a Flower, sew to secure and sew to top of Toe section.

Finishing
Pass Heel strap through lp formed on Toe section. Sew button to side edge of row 5 of Heel. ●

Plum Pretty

Skill Level

 EASY

Finished Sizes

Instructions given fit size small; changes for medium and large are in [ ].

Finished Measurements

2 inches wide x 3 inches long *(small)* [2 inches wide x 3½ inches long *(medium)*, 2 inches wide x 4 inches long *(large)*]

Materials

- Light (light worsted) weight alpaca/rayon yarn:
  1¾ oz/219 yds/50g each purple and gold
- Size C/2/2.75mm crochet hook or size needed to obtain gauge
- Yarn needle

Gauge

5 sc = 1 inch; 4 sc rnds = ½ inch

Pattern Notes

Weave in loose ends as work progresses.

Join with slip stitch as indicated unless otherwise stated.

Chain-2 at beginning of round counts as first half double crochet unless otherwise stated.

Special Stitch

Treble crochet cluster (tr cl): Ch 4, *yo twice, insert hook in indicated st, [yo, draw through 2 lps on hook] twice, sk next st, rep from * 5 [6, 6] times *(7 [8, 8] lps on hook)*, yo, draw through all 7 [8, 8] lps on hook, ch 5, sc in next unworked st.

Slippers

Sole

Make 2 each purple & gold.

Rnd 1 (RS): Ch 10 [12, 14], sc in 2nd ch from hook, sc in each of next 3 [4, 5] chs, hdc in each of next 2 [3, 4] chs, dc in each of next 2 chs, 6 dc in last ch, working on opposite side of foundation ch, dc in each of next 2 chs, hdc in each of next 2 [3, 4] chs, sc in each of next 4 [5, 6] chs, **join** *(see Pattern Notes)* in beg sc. *(22 [26, 30] sts)*

Rnd 2: Ch 1, 2 sc in same st as beg ch-1, sc in each of next 2 [3, 4] sts, hdc in each of next 4 [5, 6] sts, dc in next st, 2 dc in each of next 6 sts, dc in next st, hdc in each of next 4 [5, 6] sts, sc in each of next 2 [3, 4] sts, 2 sc in last st, join in beg sc. *(30 [34, 38] sts)*

Rnd 3: Ch 1, sc in same st as beg ch-1, 2 sc in next st, sc in each of next 1 [2, 2] st(s), hdc in each of next 6 [7, 9] sts, [hdc in next st, 2 hdc in next st] 6 times, hdc in each of next 6 [7, 9] sts, sc in each of next 1 [2, 2] st(s), 2 sc in next st, sc in last st, join in beg sc. *(38 [42, 46] sts)*

Rnd 4: Ch 1, sc in same st as beg ch-1, hdc in next st, 2 hdc in next st, hdc in each of next 6 [8, 10] sts, sc in next st, [sc in each of next 2 sts, 2 sc in next st] 6 times, sc in next st, hdc in each of next 6 [8, 10] sts, 2 hdc in next st, hdc in next st, sc in last st, join in beg sc. Fasten off. *(46 [50, 54] sts)*

Assembly

Holding 1 each purple and gold Sole with WS facing, work **running stitch** *(see illustration)* through both thicknesses around rnd 4.

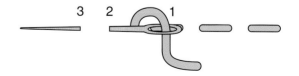

Running Stitch

Upper Shoe
Make 2.

Rnd 1: With gold Sole on top, join purple in **back lp** *(see Stitch Guide)* at center back, ch 1, sc in back lp of each st around, join in beg sc. *(46 [50, 54] sc)*

Rnd 2: Ch 2 *(see Pattern Notes)*, hdc in same st as beg ch-2, sk next st, [2 hdc in next st, sk next st] around, **change color** *(see Stitch Guide)* to gold, join in 2nd ch of beg ch-2, drop purple to WS. *(46 [50, 54] hdc)*

Rnd 3: Sl st in sp between beg ch-2 and next hdc, ch 2, hdc in same sp as beg ch-2, [2 hdc in sp between next 2 hdc] around, join in beg ch-2, sl st in next hdc, change color to purple. Fasten off gold. *(46 [50, 54] hdc)*

Rnd 4: Working in sp between groups of 2-hdc sts *(not between sts as previously done)*, insert hook in sp between groups of 2 hdc of rnd 6, yo, draw up a lp, ch 2, hdc in same sp as beg ch-2, [sk next 2 gold sts of rnd 7, 2 hdc in sp between groups of 2 hdc of rnd 6] around, join in beg ch-2. *(46 [50, 54] hdc)*

Rnd 5: Ch 1, sc in each of next 17 [18, 20] sts, working in back lp, dc in each of next 12 [14, 14] sts, working in both lps, sc in each of next 17 [18, 20] sts, join in beg sc. *(46 [50, 54] sts)*

Rnd 6: Ch 1, sc in each of next 17 [18, 20] sts, ch 4, **tr cl** *(see Special Stitch)*, sc in each of next 16 [17, 19] sts, join in beg sc. *(34 [36, 40] sc, 1 tr cl)*

Rnd 7: Ch 1, sc in each of next 17 [18, 20] sts, ch 7, sk tr cl, sc in next sc, sc in each of next 16 [17, 19] sts, join in beg sc. Fasten off. ●

Ballet Baby

Skill Level

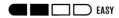 ■■□□ EASY

Finished Sizes

Instructions given fit size small; changes for medium and large are in [ ].

Finished Measurements

2 inches wide x 3 inches long *(small)* [2 inches wide x 3½ inches long *(medium)*, 2 inches wide x 4 inches long *(large)*]

Materials

- Bulky (chunky) weight nylon/acrylic yarn:
  3½ oz/150 yds/100g rose
- Medium (worsted) weight acrylic yarn:
  1 oz/50 yds/28g cream
- Size E/4/3.5mm crochet hook or size needed to obtain gauge
- Tapestry needle

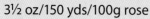

Gauge

5 sc = 1 inch; 6 rnds = 1 inch

Pattern Notes

Weave in loose ends as work progresses.

Join with slip stitch as indicated unless otherwise stated.

Chain-2 at beginning of round **does not** count as half double crochet unless otherwise stated.

Special Stitch

Surface slip stitch (surface sl st):
Insert hook RS to WS, holding yarn on WS, draw up a lp and draw through to RS, insert hook in next st, yo, draw up a lp and draw through st on hook.

Slipper
Make 2.

Rnd 1 (RS): Beg at bottom of sole, ch 9 [11, 13], sc in 2nd ch from hook, sc in each of next 4 [6, 8] chs, hdc in each of next 2 chs, 6 hdc in last ch, working on opposite side of foundation ch, hdc in each of next 2 chs, sc in each of next 5 [7, 9] chs, **join** *(see Pattern Notes)* in beg sc. *(20 [24, 28] sts)*

Rnd 2: Ch 1, sc in first st, sc in each of next 4 [6, 7] sts, hdc in each of next 2 sts, 2 hdc in each of next 6 sts, hdc in each of next 2 sts, sc in each of next 5 [7, 8] sts, join in beg sc. *(26 [30, 34] sts)*

Rnd 3: Ch 1, sc in first st, 2 sc in next st, hdc in each of next 5 [7, 9] sts, [hdc in next st, 2 hdc in next st] 6 times, hdc in each of next 5 [7, 9] sts, 2 sc in next st, sc in last st, join in beg sc. *(34 [38, 40] sts)*

Rnds 4 & 5: Ch 1, sc in each st around, join in beg sc.

Rnd 6: Ch 2 *(see Pattern Notes)*, hdc in same st as beg ch-2, hdc in each of next 4 [6, 8] sts, [dc in next st, dc dec in next 2 sts] 8 times, hdc in each of next 5 [7, 9] sts, join in beg hdc. *(26 [30, 34] sts)*

Rnd 7: Ch 1, hdc in first st, hdc in each of next 6 [8, 10] sts, [dc dec in next 2 sts] 6 times, hdc in each of next 7 [9, 11] sts, join in beg hdc. *(20 [24, 28] sts)*

Rnd 8: Ch 1, sc in each of next 7 [9, 11] sts, ch 4, sk next 6 sts, sc in each of next 7 [9, 11] sts, join in beg sc. Fasten off.

Trim

Rnd 1: Starting at center back of rnd 7, with cream, **surface sl st** *(see Special Stitch)* in each st around, join in beg sl st. Fasten off.

Join a length of cream on outer front edge over Trim and tie ends in a bow. ●

Purple Passion

Skill Level
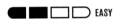 EASY

Finished Sizes
Instructions given fit size small; changes for medium and large are in [ ].

Finished Measurements
2 inches wide x 3 inches long *(small)* [2 inches wide x 3½ inches long *(medium)*, 2 inches wide x 4 inches long *(large)*]

Materials
- Medium (worsted) weight cotton yarn:

  4 MEDIUM

    2 oz/100 yds/56g dark purple
    35 yds cream
    2 yds magenta
- Size F/5/3.75mm crochet hook or size needed to obtain gauge
- Yarn needle

Gauge
4 sc = 1 inch; 5 rnds = 1 inch

Pattern Notes
Weave in loose ends as work progresses.

Join with slip stitch as indicated unless otherwise stated.

Slipper
Make 2.

Size Small Only
Rnd 1 (RS): Beg at bottom of sole, with purple, ch 8, sc in 2nd ch from hook, sc in each of next 2 chs, hdc in each of next 3 chs, 6 hdc in last ch, working on opposite side of foundation ch, hdc in each of next 3 chs, sc in each of next 3 chs, **join** *(see Pattern Notes)* in beg sc. *(18 sts)*

Sizes Medium & Large Only
Rnd [1] (RS): With purple, ch [10, 12], sc in 2nd ch from hook, sc in each of next [3, 3] chs, sl st in each of next 2 chs, sc in each of next [2, 4] chs, 6 hdc in last ch, working on opposite side of foundation ch, sc in each of next [2, 4] chs, sl st in each of next 2 chs, sc in each of next [4, 4] chs, **join** *(see Pattern Notes)* in beg sc. *([22, 26 sts])*

All Sizes

Rnd 2: Ch 1, 2 sc in first st, sc in each of next 5 [7, 9] sts, 2 hdc in each of next 6 sts, sc in each of next 5 [7, 9] sts, 2 sc in next st, join in beg sc. *(26 [30, 34] sts)*

Rnd 3: Ch 1, 2 sc in each of next 2 sts, sc in each of next 5 [7, 9] sts, [hdc in next st, 2 hdc in next st] 6 times, sc in each of next 5 [7, 9] sts, 2 sc in each of next 2 sts, join in beg sc. *(36 [40, 44] sts)*

Rnd 4: Ch 1, working in **back lp** *(see Stitch Guide)*, sc in each st around, join in beg sc. *(36 [40, 44] sts)*

Rnd 5: Ch 1, sc in each of next 12 [14, 16] sts, [dc in next st, **dc dec** *(see Stitch Guide)* in next 2 sts] 4 times, sc in each of next 12 sts, join in beg sc. *(32 [36, 40] sts)*

Rnd 6: Ch 1, sc in each of next 10 [12, 14] sts, [**hdc dec** *(see Stitch Guide)* in next 2 sts] 6 times, sc in each of next 10 [12, 14] sts, join in beg sc. *(26 [30, 34] sts)*

Rnd 7: Ch 1, sc in each of next 10 [12, 14] sts, [**sc dec** *(see Stitch Guide)* in next 2 sts] 3 times, sc in each of next 10 [12, 14] sts, join in beg sc. Fasten off. *(23 [27, 31] sts)*

Rnd 8: Join cream at center back of rnd 7, sl st in each st around. Fasten off.

Ruffle
Make 2.

Row 1: With cream, ch 15, sl st in 4th ch from hook, (sl st, ch 4, sl st) in each ch across to last ch, sl st in last ch, (ch 4, sl st) twice in same last ch, working on opposite side of foundation ch, (sl st, ch 4, sl st) in each ch across to last ch, (sl st, ch 4, sl st) in same ch as beg sts. Fasten off.

Assembly
With yarn needle and length of cream, sew each Ruffle across center front of each Slipper.

Flower
Make 2.

Rnd 1: With magenta, ch 2, 4 sc in 2nd ch from hook, join in beg sc, leaving a 6-inch length of yarn, fasten off.

Sew a Flower positioned at center of Ruffle on each outer edge of each Slipper. ●

Preppy

Skill Level

 **EASY**

Finished Sizes

Instructions given fit size small; changes for medium and large are in [ ].

Finished Measurements

2 inches wide x 3 inches long *(small)* [2 inches wide x 3½ inches long *(medium)*, 2 inches wide x 4 inches long *(large)*]

Materials

- Light (light worsted) weight acrylic yarn:
  - 2 oz/144 yds/56g olive
  - 1 oz/72 yds/28g cream
- Size C/2/2.75mm crochet hook or size needed to obtain gauge
- Tapestry needle
- Sewing needle
- Sewing thread
- 10mm shank buttons: 4

Gauge

6 sc rnds = 1 inch; 5 sc = 1 inch

Pattern Notes

Weave in loose ends as work progresses.

Join with slip stitch as indicated unless otherwise stated.

Shoe

Make 2.

Rnd 1 (RS): Beg with sole, with olive, ch 8 [10, 12], sc in 2nd ch from hook, sc in each of next 5 [7, 9] chs, 4 sc in last ch, working on opposite side of foundation ch, sc in each of next 6 [8, 10] chs, **join** (see Pattern Notes) in beg sc. (16 [20, 24] sts)

Rnd 2: Ch 1, 2 sc in first st, sc in each of next 5 [7, 9] sts, 2 dc in each of next 4 sts, sc in each of next 5 [7, 9] sts, 2 sc in last st, join in beg sc. (22 [26, 30] sts)

Rnd 3: Ch 1, 2 sc in each of next 2 sts, sc in each of next 7 [9, 11] sts, 2 hdc in each of next 4 sts, sc in each of next 7 [9, 11] sts, 2 sc in each of next 2 sts, join in beg sc. (30 [34, 38] sts)

Rnd 4: Ch 1, sc in first st, 2 sc in next st, sc in next st, hdc in each of next 8 [10, 12] sts, [2 hdc in next st, hdc in next st] 4 times, hdc in each of next 8 [10, 12] sts, sc in next st, 2 sc in next st, sc in next st, join in beg sc. (36 [40, 44] sts)

Rnd 5: Working in **back lp** (see Stitch Guide) of sts, ch 1, sc in each of next 11 [13, 15] sts, hdc in each of next 2 sts, dc in each of next 10 sts, hdc in each of next 2 sts, sc in each of next 11 [13, 15] sts, join in beg sc, join cream. Fasten off olive. (36 [40, 44] sts)

Rnd 6: Ch 1, sc in each of next 11 [13, 15] sts, hdc in each of next 2 sts, dc in each of next 10 sts, hdc in each of next 2 sts, sc in each of next 11 [13, 15] sts, join in beg sc. (36 [40, 44] sts)

Rnd 7: Ch 1, sc in each of next 11 [13, 15] sts, **hdc dec** (see Stitch Guide) in next 2 sts, dc in each of next 10 sts, hdc dec in next 2 sts, sc in each of next 11 [13, 15] sts, join in beg sc. (34 [38, 42] sts)

Rnd 8: Ch 1, sc in each of next 11 [13, 15] sts, sl st in next st, ch 3, [yo, insert hook in back lp of next st, yo, draw up lp, yo, draw through 2 lps on hook] 10 times (11 lps on hook), yo, draw through all lps on hook, ch 4, sl st in next unworked st, sc in each of next 11 [13, 15] sts, join in beg sc. Fasten off.

Strap
Make 2.

Row 1: With cream, ch 15, sc in 4th ch from hook *(first buttonhole)*, sc in each of next 8 chs, sl st in last ch *(2nd buttonhole)*. Fasten off.

With sewing needle and thread, sew a button to each side of Shoe. Button each end of Strap to buttons. ●

Little Man

Skill Level
 **EASY**

Finished Sizes
Instructions given fit size small; changes for medium and large are in [ ].

Finished Measurements
2 inches wide x 3 inches long *(small)* [2 inches wide x 3½ inches long *(medium)*, 2 inches wide x 4 inches long *(large)*]

Materials

- Medium (worsted) weight acrylic/ wool/rayon yarn:
  3 oz/200 yds/100g dark gold fleck
- Size F/5/3.75mm crochet hook or size needed to obtain gauge
- Tapestry needle
- Sewing needle
- Brown sewing thread
- 14mm brown buttons: 4

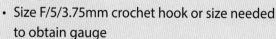

Gauge

4 rnds = 1 inch; 4 sts = 1 inch

Pattern Notes

Weave in loose ends as work progresses.

Join with slip stitch as indicated unless otherwise stated.

Chain-2 at beginning of round **does not** count as first half double crochet unless otherwise stated.

Shoe

Make 2.

Rnd 1 (RS): Beg with sole, ch 8 [10, 12] sc in 2nd ch from hook, sc in each of next 3 [3, 4] chs, hdc in each of next 1 [3, 3] ch(s), dc in each of next 1 [1, 2] ch(s), 6 dc in last ch, working on opposite side of foundation ch, dc in each of next 1 [1, 2] ch(s), hdc in each of next 1 [3, 3] ch(s), sc in each of next 4 [4, 5] chs, **join** (see Pattern Notes) in beg sc. (18 [22, 26] sts)

Rnd 2: Ch 1, 2 sc in same st as beg ch-1, sc in each of next 3 [3, 4] sts, hdc in each of next 1 [3, 3] st(s), dc in each of next 1 [1, 2] st(s), 2 dc in each of next 6 sts, dc in next 1 [1, 2] st(s), hdc in each of next 1 [3, 3] st(s), sc in each of next 3 [3, 4] sts, 2 sc in last st, join in beg sc. (26 [30, 34] sts)

Rnd 3: Ch 1, sc in same st, 2 sc in next st, sc in each of next 2 [2, 3] sts, hdc in each of next 3 [5, 6] sts, [hdc in next st, 2 hdc in next st] 6 times, hdc in each of next 3 [5, 6] sts, sc in each of next 2 [2, 3] sts, 2 sc in next st, sc in last st, join in beg sc. (34 [38, 42] sts)

Rnd 4: Ch 1, working in **back lp** (see Stitch Guide) of sts, sc in each of next 12 [14, 16] sts, **sc dec** (see Stitch Guide) in next 2 sts, sc in each of next 6 sts, sc dec in next 2 sts, sc in each of next 12 [14, 16] sts, join in beg sc. (32 [36, 40] sts)

Continued on page 30

Mock Crocs

Skill Level
 EASY

Finished Sizes
Instructions given fit size small; changes for medium and large are in [ ].

Finished Measurements
2 inches wide x 3 inches long *(small)* [2 inches wide x 3½ inches long *(medium)*, 2 inches wide x 4 inches long *(large)*]

Materials

- Medium (worsted) weight acrylic yarn:
   2 oz/100 yds/56g gray heather
   1 oz/50 yds/28g red
- Size D/3/3.25mm crochet hook or size needed to obtain gauge
- Tapestry needle
- Stitch markers: 4

Gauge
5 sc rnds = 1 inch; 6 sc sts = 1 inch

Pattern Notes
Weave in loose ends as work progresses.

Join with slip stitch as indicated unless otherwise stated.

Chain-2 at beginning of row **does not** count as first half double crochet unless otherwise stated.

Special Stitch
Surface slip stitch (surface sl st): Insert hook RS to WS, holding yarn on WS, draw up a lp and draw through to RS, insert hook in next st, yo, draw up a lp and draw through st on hook.

Crocs

Sole
Make 4.

Rnd 1 (RS): With gray heather, ch 8 [10, 12], 2 sc in 2nd ch from hook, sc in each of next 5 [7, 9] chs, 4 sc in last ch, working on opposite side of foundation ch, sc in each of next 5 [7, 9] chs, 2 sc in last ch, **join** *(see Pattern Notes)* in beg sc. *(18 [22, 26] sc)*

Rnd 2: Ch 1, 2 sc in first st, sc in each of next 6 [8, 10] sts, 2 dc in each of next 4 sts, sc in each of next 6 [8, 10] sts, 2 sc in last st, join in beg sc. *(24 [28, 32] sts)*

Rnd 3: Ch 1, sc in first st, 2 sc in next st, sc in each of next 5 [7, 9] sts, hdc in next st, [dc in next st, 2 dc in next st] 4 times, hdc in next st, sc in each of next 5 [7, 9] sts, 2 sc in next st, sc in last st, join in beg sc. *(30 [34, 38] sts)*

Rnd 4: Ch 1, sc in first st, 2 sc in next st, sc in next st, 2 sc in next st, sc in each of next 5 [7, 9] sts, [sc in next each of next 2 sts, 2 sc in next st] 4 times, place stitch marker in first sc of next sc group, sc in each of next 5 [7, 9] sts, [2 sc in next st, sc in next st] twice, join in beg sc. Fasten off. *(38 [42, 46] sts)*

Assembly
With WS of 2 Soles facing and working through both thicknesses with red, **surface sl st** *(see Special Stitch)* through both thicknesses in each st around, join in beg sl st. Fasten off. Join rem 2 Soles in same manner.

Toe
Make 2.

Row 1 (RS): Join gray heather in marked st on Sole, remove stitch marker, **ch 2** *(see Pattern Notes)*, hdc in same st as beg ch-2, [hdc in next st, ch 1, sk next st]

4 times, hdc in each of next 2 sts, [ch 1, sk next st, hdc in next st] 4 times, hdc in next st, turn. *(20 sts)*

Row 2: Ch 2, hdc in each hdc across, turn. *(20 hdc)*

Row 3: Ch 2, hdc in same st as beg ch-2, [hdc in next st, **hdc dec** *(see Stitch Guide)* in next 2 sts] 6 times, hdc in next st. Fasten off gray, turn. *(14 sts)*

Row 4: Join red, ch 2, hdc in same st as beg ch-2, [hdc dec in next 2 sts] 6 times, hdc in next st, join gray. Fasten off red, turn. *(8 sts)*

Row 5: Ch 2, hdc in same st as beg ch-2, [hdc dec in next 2 sts] 3 times, hdc in next st, turn. *(5 sts)*

Row 6: Ch 1, sc in first st, **sc dec** *(see Stitch Guide)* in next 3 sts, sc in last st. Fasten off. *(3 sts)*

Strap
Make 2.

Row 1 (RS): Join gray in side edge of row 2 of Toe, ch 18 [20, 20], sl st in opposite side of row 2 of Toe, sl st in top edge of row 2, turn.

Row 2: Working in **back bar of ch** *(see illustration)*, sc in each ch across, sl st in top of row 2 of Toe on opposite side. Fasten off. ●

Back Bar of Chain

Serenity

Skill Level
 EASY

Finished Sizes
Instructions given fit size small; changes for medium and large are in [ ].

Finished Measurements
2 inches wide x 3 inches long *(small)* [2 inches wide x 3½ inches long *(medium)*, 2 inches wide x 4 inches long *(large)*]

Materials

- Medium (worsted) weight superwash merino wool/nylon yarn:
  3½ oz/190 yds/100g purple/green/blue/gray variegated
- Size E/4/3.5mm crochet hook or size needed to obtain gauge
- Tapestry needle

Gauge
7 fpdc = 1½ inches

Pattern Notes
Weave in loose ends as work progresses.

Join with slip stitch as indicated unless otherwise stated.

Chain-2 at beginning of round **does not** count as first stitch unless otherwise stated.

Chain-3 at beginning of round counts as first double crochet unless otherwise stated.

Special Stitches
Front post double crochet decrease (fpdc dec): [Yo, insert hook front to back to front around vertical post of next st, yo, draw through 2 lps on hook] twice, yo, draw through all 3 lps on hook.

Front post double crochet decrease in next 3 stitches (fpdc dec in next 3 sts): [Yo, insert hook front to back to front again around vertical post, yo, draw up a lp, yo, draw through 2 lps on hook] 3 times, yo, draw through all 4 lps on hook.

Beginning crocodile stitch (beg crocodile st): Ch 3, 4 dc down post of first dc of previous rnd, ch 1, 5 dc up next dc post.

Crocodile stitch (crocodile st): 5 dc down next dc post, ch 1, 5 dc up next dc post.

Boot
Make 2.

Rnd 1 (RS): Beg with sole, ch 11 [13, 15], sc in 2nd ch from hook, sc in next 2 [3, 4] chs, hdc in each of next 4 [2, 3] chs, dc in each of next 2 [5, 5] chs, 6 dc in last ch, working on opposite side of foundation ch, dc in each of next 2 [5, 5] chs, hdc in each of next 4 [2, 3] chs, sc in each of next 3 [4, 5] chs, **join** *(see Pattern Notes)* in beg sc. *(24 [28, 32] sts)*

Rnd 2: Ch 1, 2 sc in same st as beg ch-1, sc in each of next 2 sts, hdc in each of next 4 [4, 5] sts, dc in each of next 2 [4, 5] sts, 2 dc in each of next 6 sts, dc in each of next 2 [4, 5] sts, hdc in each of next 4 [4, 5] sts, sc in each of next 2 sts, 2 sc in last st, join in beg sc. *(32 [36, 40] sts)*

Rnd 3: Ch 1, sc in same st as beg ch-1, 2 sc in next st, sc in each of next 2 sts, hdc in each of next 6 [8, 10] sts, [hdc in next st, 2 hdc in next st] 6 times, hdc in each of next 6 [8, 10] sts, sc in each of next 2 sts, 2 sc in next st, sc in last st, join in beg sc. *(40 [44, 48] sts)*

Rnd 4: Ch 2 *(see Pattern Notes)*, working in **back lp** *(see Stitch Guide)* of sts, dc in each st around, join in first dc. *(40 [44, 48] dc)*

Rnd 5: Ch 2, **fpdc** *(see Stitch Guide)* in each of next 11 [13, 15] sts, [fpdc in next st, **fpdc dec** *(see Special Stitches)* in next 2 sts] 6 times, fpdc in each of next 11 [13, 15] sts, join in first fpdc. *(34 [38, 42] sts)*

Rnd 6: Ch 2, fpdc in each of next 11 [13, 15] sts, [fpdc dec in next 2 sts] 6 times, fpdc in each of next 11 [13, 15] sts, join in first fpdc. *(28 [32, 36] sts)*

Rnd 7: Ch 2, fpdc in each of next 11 [13, 15] sts, fpdc dec in next 2 sts, fpdc in each of next 2 sts, fpdc dec in next 2 sts, fpdc in each of next 11 [13, 15] sts, join in first fpdc. *(26 [30, 34] sts)*

Rnd 8: Ch 2, fpdc in each of next 11 [13, 15] sts, **fpdc dec in next 3 sts** *(see Special Stitches)*, fpdc in each of next 11 [13, 15] sts, join in first fpdc. *(24 [28, 32] sts)*

Rnd 9: Ch 3 *(see Pattern Notes)*, dc in same st as beg ch-3, sk next st, [2 dc in next st, sk next st] around, join in 3rd ch of beg ch-3. *(24 [28, 32] sts)*

Rnd 10: Beg crocodile st *(see Special Stitches)*, [sk next 2-dc group, **crocodile st** *(see Special Stitches)* in next 2-dc group] around, join in center of first crocodile st. *(6 [7, 8] crocodile sts)*

Rnd 11: Ch 3, dc in same st as beg ch-3, 2 dc in center of next unworked 2-dc group, [2 dc in center of next crocodile st, 2 dc in center of next unworked 2-dc group] around, join in beg ch-3, sl st in each of next 2 dc *(this is the 2-dc group that does not have a crocodile st directly below)*.

Note: Use care on the following rnds when working rep of rnd 10 to stagger crocodile sts.

Rnds 12–15: [Rep rnds 10 and 11] twice.

Rnd 16: Rep rnd 10. Fasten off. ●

Rootin' Tootin' Cowboy

Skill Level

 EASY

Finished Sizes

Instructions given fit size small; changes for medium and large are in [ ].

Finished Measurements

2 inches wide x 3 inches long *(small)* [2 inches wide x 3½ inches long *(medium)*, 2 inches wide x 4 inches long *(large)*]

Materials

- Medium (worsted) weight acrylic yarn:
    3½ oz/180 yds/100g each brown and tan
- Size F/5/3.75mm crochet hook or size needed to obtain gauge
- Tapestry needle
- Sewing needle
- Sewing thread
- 28mm red star buttons: 2

Gauge

6 sts = 1½ inches

Pattern Notes

Weave in loose ends as work progresses.

Join with slip stitch as indicated unless otherwise stated.

Chain-2 at beginning of round **does not** count as first half double crochet unless otherwise stated.

Chain-2 at beginning of round **does not** count as first double crochet unless otherwise stated.

Boot

Make 2.

Rnd 1 (RS): With brown, beg with sole, ch 8 [10, 12], sc in 2nd ch from hook, sc in each of next 2 [3, 4] chs, hdc in each of next 2 [3, 3] chs, dc in each of next 1 [1, 2] ch(s), 4 dc in last ch, working on opposite side of foundation ch, dc in each of next 1 [1, 2] ch(s), hdc in each of next 2 [3, 3] chs, sc in each of next 3 [4, 5] chs, **join** *(see Pattern Notes)* in beg sc. *(16 [20, 24] sts)*

Rnd 2: Ch 1, 2 sc in same st, sc in each of next 3 [4, 5] sts, hdc in each of next 2 [3, 4] sts, 2 dc in each of next 4 sts, hdc in each of next 2 [3, 4] sts, sc in each of next 3 [4, 5] sts, 2 sc in last st, join in beg sc. *(22 [26, 30] sts)*

Rnd 3: Ch 1, sc in same st, 2 sc in next st, sc in each of next 1 [2, 3] st(s), hdc in each of next 6 [7, 8] sts, 2 hdc in each of next 4 sts, hdc in each of next 6 [7, 8] sts, sc in each of next 1 [2, 3] st(s), 2 sc in next st, sc in last st, join in beg sc. *(28 [32, 36] sts)*

Rnd 4: Ch 1, working in **back lp** *(see Stitch Guide)* of sts, sc in each of next 28 [32, 36] sts, **change color** *(see Stitch Guide)* to tan, join in beg sc. Fasten off brown.

Rnd 5: Ch 2 *(see Pattern Notes)*, hdc in each st around, join in beg hdc. *(28 [32, 36] sts)*

Rnd 6: Ch 1, sc in each of next 8 [10, 12] sts, [**dc dec** *(see Stitch Guide)* in next 2 sts] 6 times, sc in each of next 8 [10, 10] sts, join in beg st. *(22 [26, 30] sts)*

Rnd 7: Ch 1, sc in each of next 8 [10, 12] sts, [**sc dec** *(see Stitch Guide)* in next 2 sts] 3 times, sc in each of next 8 [10, 12] sts, join in beg st. *(19 [23, 27] sts)*

Rnd 8: Ch 2 *(see Pattern Notes)*, dc in each of next 4 [4, 4] sts, sc in each of next 4 [6, 8] sts, sc dec next 3 sts tog, sc in each of next 4 [6, 8] sts, dc in each of next 4 [4, 4] sts, join in first dc. *(17 [21, 25] sts)*

Rnd 9: Ch 2, hdc in each of next 4 [4, 4] sts, sc in each of next 9 [13, 17] sts, hdc in each of next 4 [4, 4] sts, change color to brown, join in first hdc. Fasten off tan. *(17 [21, 25] sts)*

Rnd 10: Ch 2, dc in each st around, join in beg dc.

Rnd(s) 11 [11 & 12, 11 & 12]: Rep rnd 10. *(17 [21, 25] sts)*

Rnd 12 [13, 13]: Ch 1, sc in each of next 1 [2, 2] st(s), sk next 2 sts, 5 dc in next st, sk next 2 sts, sc in each of next 5 [7, 11] sts, sk next 2 sts, 5 dc in next st, sk next 2 sts, sc in each of last 1 [2, 2] st(s), change color to tan, join in first sc. Fasten off brown. *(17 [21, 25] sts)*

Rnd 13 [14, 14]: Ch 1, sc in each of next 3 [4, 4] sts, 2 sc in next st, sc in each of next 9 [11, 15] sts, 2 sc in next st, sc in each of next 3 [4, 4] sts, join in beg sc. *(19 [23, 27] sts)*

Finishing
Sew a star button centered on rnd below 5-dc sts on outer edge of each Boot. ●

Tropical Bright

Skill Level

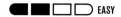 EASY

Finished Sizes

Instructions given fit size small; changes for medium and large are in [ ].

Finished Measurements

2 inches wide x 3 inches long (small) [2 inches wide x 3½ inches long (medium), 2 inches wide x 4 inches long (large)]

Materials

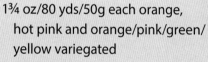

- Medium (worsted) weight cotton yarn:
  1¾ oz/80 yds/50g each orange, hot pink and orange/pink/green/yellow variegated
- Size E/4/3.5mm crochet hook or size needed to obtain gauge
- Tapestry needle
- Stitch markers

Gauge

4 sc = 1 inch; 4 rnds = 1 inch

Pattern Notes

Weave in loose ends as work progresses.

Join with slip stitch as indicated unless otherwise stated.

Do not join rounds unless otherwise indicated. Use stitch marker to mark rounds, moving marker as work progresses.

Boot

Make 2.

Rnd 1 (RS): Beg with sole and orange, ch 9 [11, 13], sc in 2nd ch from hook, sc in each of next 2 [2, 3] chs, hdc in each of next 3 [4, 2] chs, dc in each of next 1 [2, 5] ch(s), 6 dc in last ch, working on opposite side of foundation ch, dc in each of next 1 [2, 5] ch(s), hdc in each of next 3 [4, 2] chs, sc in each of next 3 [3, 4] chs, **join** (see Pattern Notes) in beg sc. (20 [24, 28] sts)

Rnd 2: Ch 1, 2 sc in same st, sc in each of next 2 [2, 2] sts, hdc in each of next 3 [4, 4] sts, dc in each of next 1 [2, 4] st(s), 2 dc in each of next 6 sts, dc in each of next 1 [2, 4] st(s), hdc in each of next 3 [4, 4] sts, sc in each of next 2 [2, 2] sts, 2 sc in last st, join in beg sc. (28 [32, 36] sts)

Rnd 3: Ch 1, sc in same st, 2 sc in next st, sc in each of next 2 [2, 2] sts, hdc in each of next 4 [6, 8] sts, [hdc in next st, 2 hdc in next st] 6 times, hdc in each of next 4 [6, 8] sts, sc in each of next 2 [2, 2] sts, 2 sc in next st, sc in last st, join in beg sc. (36 [40, 44] sts)

Rnd 4: Ch 1, working in **back lps** (see Stitch Guide), sc in each st around, change color to hot pink, join in beg sc. Fasten off orange. (36 [40, 44] sts)

Rnd 5: Ch 1, sc in each st around, join in beg sc. (36 [40, 44] sts)

Rnd 6: Ch 1, sc in each of next 9 [11, 13] sts, [sc in next st, **sc dec** (see Stitch Guide) in next 2 sts] 6 times, sc in each of next 9 [11, 13] sts, **place stitch marker, do not join** (see Pattern Notes). (30 [34, 38] sts)

Rnd 7: Sc in each of next 9 [11, 13] sts, [sc dec in next 2 sts] 6 times, sc in each of next 9 [11, 13] sts. (24 [28, 32] sts)

Rnd 8: Sc in each of next 9 [11, 13] sts, [sc dec in next 2 sts] 3 times, sc in each of next 9 [11, 13] sts. (21 [25, 29] sts)

Rnd 9: Sc in each of next 7 [9, 11] sts, sc dec in next 2 sts, sc dec next 3 sts tog, sc dec in next 2 sts, sc in each of next 7 [9, 11] sts, join in next sc, remove marker. *(17 [21, 25] sts)*

Rnds 10–17: Ch 1, sc in each st around, join in beg sc.

Right Boot

Rnd 18 (RS): Join orange in center sc of outer side edge of Right Boot, ch 1, sc in each st around, join in beg sc, turn. *(17 [21, 25] sc)*

Row 19: Now working in rows, ch 1, working in back lp of sts, sc in each of next 17 [21, 25] sts, turn.

Rows 20–23: Ch 1, sc in each of next 17 [21, 25] sts, turn. At the end of row 23, fasten off.

Left Boot

Rnd 18: Join orange in center sc of outer side edge of Left Boot, ch 1, sc in each st around, join in beg sc, turn. *(17 [21, 25] sc)*

Rows 19–23: Rep rows 19–23 of Right Boot.

Finishing

Make 2 pompoms per Boot. Working with variegated, cut 6-inch length for each pompom and set aside. Wrap variegated around 2 fingers 25 times. Carefully remove yarn from fingers. Holding winding of yarn closed in hand, tie 6-inch length of yarn tightly around center of hank of yarn, knot ends tog 3 times. Cut opposite ends of hank open at each end and trim even. Fluff pompom and trim if needed.

Cut 24-inch length of variegated, fold in half, starting at outer edge of Boot, weave in and out of rnd 18, leaving 4-inch length on each end. Attach pompom to each end of tie. Secure ends with double knot. ●

On the Slopes

Skill Level

 EASY

Finished Sizes

Instructions given fit size small; changes for medium and large are in [ ].

Finished Measurements

2 inches wide x 3 inches long *(small)* [2 inches wide x 3½ inches long *(medium)*, 2 inches wide x 4 inches long *(large)*]

Materials

- Medium (worsted) weight acrylic yarn:
  2 oz/100 yds/56g white
  1 oz/50 yds/28g each bright green and gray
- Size F/5/3.75mm crochet hook or size needed to obtain gauge
- Tapestry needle

Gauge

4 rnds = 1 inch; 4 sts = 1 inch

Pattern Notes

Weave in loose ends as work progresses.

Join with slip stitch as indicated unless otherwise stated.

Chain-2 at beginning of round **does not** count as first double crochet unless otherwise stated.

Bootie

Make 2.

Rnd 1 (RS): With white, beg with sole, ch 8 [10, 12], sc in 2nd ch from hook, sc in each of next 2 [3, 4] chs, hdc in each of next 2 [2, 3] chs, dc in each of next 1 [2, 2] ch(s), 6 dc in last ch, working on opposite side of foundation ch, dc in next ch, hdc in each of next 2 [2, 3] chs, sc in each of next 3 [4, 5] chs, **join** *(see Pattern Notes)* in beg sc. *(18 [22, 26] sts)*

Rnd 2: Ch 1, 2 sc in same st, sc in each of next 2 [4, 5] sts, hdc in each of next 3 [3, 4] sts, 2 dc in each of next 6 sts, hdc in each of next 3 [3, 4] sts, sc in each of next 2 [4, 5] sts, 2 sc in last st, join in beg sc. *(26 [30, 34] sts)*

Rnd 3: Ch 1, sc in same st, 2 sc in next st, sc in each of next 5 [7, 9] sts, [sc in next st, 2 sc in next st] 6 times, sc in each of next 5 [7, 9] sts, 2 sc in next st, sc in last st, join in beg sc. *(34 [38, 42] sts)*

Rnd 4: Ch 1, working in **back lps** *(see Stitch Guide)*, sc in each st around, join in beg sc.

Rnd 5: Ch 2 *(see Pattern Notes)*, dc in each of next 5 [7, 9] sts, [dc in next st, **dc dec** *(see Stitch Guide)* in next 2 sts] 8 times, dc in each of next 5 [7, 9] sts, join in beg dc. *(26 [30, 34] sts)*

Rnd 6: Ch 2, dc in each of next 5 [6, 7] sts, [dc dec in next 2 sts] 8 [9, 10] times, dc in each of next 5 [6, 7] sts, join in beg dc. *(18 [21, 24] sts)*

Rnd 7: Ch 2, dc in each dc around, join in beg dc.

Rnd 8: Ch 1, sc in each st around, join in beg sc.

Rnd 9: Ch 1, sc in each st around, **change color** *(see Stitch Guide)* to green, join in beg sc. Fasten off white.

Rnd 10: Ch 1, [sc in each of next 2 sc, sk previous rnd, insert hook in st 2 rnds directly below, yo, draw up a lp, yo, draw through 2 lps on hook] around, join in beg sc.

Rnd 11: Ch 1, sc in each sc around, draw up lp of gray, join in beg sc. Fasten off green.

Rnd 12: Sl st in next st, ch 1, sc in same st as beg ch-1, sc in next st, insert hook in st 2 rnds directly below, yo, draw up a lp, yo, draw through 2 lps on hook, [sc in each of next 2 sc, sk previous rnd, insert hook in st 2 rnds directly below, yo, draw up a lp, yo, draw through 2 lps on hook] around, join in beg sc.

Rnd 13: Ch 1, sc in each sc around, draw up lp of white, join in beg sc. Fasten off gray.

Rnd 14: Sl st in next st, ch 1, sc in same st as beg ch-1, sc in next st, insert hook in st 2 rnds directly below, yo, draw up a lp, yo, draw through 2 lps on hook, [sc in each of next 2 sc, sk previous rnd, insert hook in st 2 rnds directly below, yo, draw up a lp, yo, draw through 2 lps on hook] around, join in beg sc.

Rnd 15: Ch 1, sc in each st around, join in beg sc. Fasten off. ●

Houndstooth

Skill Level
 ■■□□ EASY

Finished Sizes
Instructions given fit size small; changes for medium and large are in [ ].

Finished Measurements
2 inches wide x 3 inches long *(small)* [2 inches wide x 3½ inches long *(medium)*, 2 inches wide x 4 inches long *(large)*]

Materials

- Light (DK) weight nylon/ acrylic yarn:
    1¾ oz/178 yds/50g each black, soft white and dark gray
- Size C/2/2.75mm crochet hook or size needed to obtain gauge
- Yarn needle
- Sewing needle
- Sewing thread
- 12mm buttons: 2

Gauge
6 sc = 1 inch; 5 sc rnds = 1 inch

Pattern Notes
Weave in loose ends as work progresses.

Join with slip stitch as indicated unless otherwise stated.

Chain-2 at beginning of a round **does not** count as a double crochet unless otherwise indicated.

Boots

Sole
Make 2 each black & soft white.

Rnd 1 (RS): Ch 8 [10, 12], 2 sc in 2nd ch from hook, sc in each of next 5 [7, 9] chs, 4 sc in last ch, working on opposite side of foundation ch, sc in each of next 5 [7, 9] chs, 2 sc in last ch, **join** *(see Pattern Notes)* in beg sc. *(18 [22, 26] sc)*

Rnd 2: Ch 1, 2 sc in first st, sc in each of next 6 [8, 10] sts, 2 dc in each of next 4 sts, sc in each of next 6 [8, 10] sts, 2 sc in last st, join in beg sc. *(24 [28, 32] sts)*

Rnd 3: Ch 1, sc in first st, 2 sc in next st, sc in next st, 2 sc in next st, sc in each of next 2 [4, 6] sts, hdc in each of next 4 sts, 2 dc in each of next 4 sts, hdc in each of next 4 sts, sc in each of next 2 [4, 6] sts, 2 sc in next st, sc in next st, 2 sc in next st, sc in last st, join in beg sc. *(32 [36, 40] sts)*

Rnd 4: Ch 1, sc in each of next 2 sts, 2 sc in next st, sc in each of next 7 [9, 11] sts, hdc in each of next 2 sts, [hdc in next st, 2 hdc in next st] 4 times, hdc in each of next 2 sts, sc in each of next 7 [9, 11] sts, 2 sc in next st, sc in each of next 2 sts, join in beg sc. Fasten off. *(38 [42, 46] sts)*

Thread yarn needle with length of soft white, holding 1 each black and soft white Sole tog, sew Soles tog with **running stitch** *(see illustration)* through sts of rnd 4.

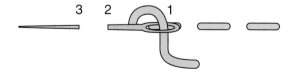

Running Stitch

Upper Boot
Make 2.

Rnd 1: Working in **back lp** (see Stitch Guide) of sts of soft white Sole, join gray in last st of rnd 4, ch 1, sc in same st as beg ch-1, sc in each of next 10 [12, 14] sts, hdc in each of next 2 sts, dc in each of next 12 sts (center front), hdc in each of next 2 sts, sc in each of next 11 [13, 15] sts, join in beg sc. (38 [42, 46] sts)

Rnd 2: Ch 1, sc in first st, sc in each of next 10 [12, 14] sts, hdc in each of next 2 sts, [dc in next st, **dc dec** (see Stitch Guide) in next 2 sts] 4 times, hdc in each of next 2 sts, sc in each of next 11 [13, 15] sts, join in beg sc. (34 [38, 42] sts)

Rnd 3: Ch 1, sc in each of next 11 [13, 15] sts, [dc dec in next 2 sts] 6 times, sc in each of next 11 [13, 15] sts, join in beg sc. (28 [32, 36] sts)

Rnd 4: Ch 1, sc in each of next 8 [10, 12] sts, **sc dec** (see Stitch Guide) in next 2 sts, [dc dec in next 2 sts] 4 times, sc dec in next 2 sts, sc in each of next 8 [10, 12] sts, join in beg sc. (22 [26, 30] sts)

Rnd 5: Ch 1, sc in each st around, join in beg sc.

Rnd 6: Join soft white, drop gray to WS of Upper Boot, ch 1, [sc in next st, dc in next st] around, join in beg sc. (22 [26, 30] sts)

Rnd 7: With gray, drop soft white to WS, **ch 2** (see Pattern Notes), dc in same sc, sc in next dc, [dc in next sc, sc in next dc] around, join in first dc.

Rnd 8: With soft white, drop gray to WS, ch 1, sc in same dc, dc in next sc, [sc in next dc, dc in next sc] around, join in beg sc.

Rnds 9–14: [Rep rnds 7 and 8 alternately] 3 times. At the end of rnd 14, join black. Fasten off gray and soft white.

Rnd 15: Ch 1, sc in each st around, join in beg sc. Fasten off.

Boot Strap
Make 2.

Row 1: With black, ch 41, sc in 2nd ch from hook, sc in each rem ch across. Fasten off. (40 sc)

Assembly
Overlap ends of Strap and sew a button centered on overlapped section. Slide Strap over Upper Boot section. If desired, with yarn needle and length of black, tack Strap to center front of Boot. ●

Dreamsicle

Skill Level

■ ■ □ □ EASY

Finished Sizes

Instructions given fit size small; changes for medium and large are in [ ].

Finished Measurements

2 inches wide x 3 inches long *(small)* [2 inches wide x 3½ inches long *(medium)*, 2 inches wide x 4 inches long *(large)*]

Materials

- Medium (worsted) weight acrylic/wool yarn:
  3½ oz/200 yds/100g gray/orange/light blue variegated
- Size F/5/3.75mm crochet hook or size needed to obtain gauge
- Tapestry needle

4 MEDIUM

Gauge

4 rnds = 1 inch; 4 sts = 1 inch

Pattern Notes

Weave in loose ends as work progresses.

Join with slip stitch as indicated unless otherwise stated.

Chain-2 at beginning of round **does not** count as first double crochet unless otherwise stated.

Chain-2 at beginning of round **does not** count as first half double crochet unless otherwise stated.

Chain-3 at beginning of round counts as first double crochet unless otherwise stated.

Bootie
Make 2.

Rnd 1 (RS): Ch 9 [11, 13], sc in 2nd ch from hook, sc in each of next 2 [3, 3] chs, hdc in each of next 2 chs, dc in each of next 2 [3, 5] chs, 6 dc in last ch, working on opposite side of foundation ch, dc in each of next 2 [3, 5] chs, hdc in each of next 2 chs, sc in each of next 3 [4, 4] chs, **join** *(see Pattern Notes)* in beg sc. *(20 [24, 28] sts)*

Rnd 2: Ch 1, 2 sc in same st as beg ch-1, sc in each of next 1 [2, 2] st(s), hdc in each of next 4 sts, dc in each of next 1 [2, 4] st(s), 2 dc in each of next 6 sts, dc in each of next 1 [2, 4] st(s), hdc in each of next 4 sts, sc in each of next 1 [2, 2] st(s), 2 sc in last st, join in beg sc. *(28 [32, 36] sts)*

Rnd 3: Ch 1, sc in same st as beg ch-1, 2 sc in next st, sc in each of next 1 [2, 2] st(s), hdc in each of next 5 [6, 8] sts, [hdc in next st, 2 hdc in next st] 6 times, hdc in each of next 5 [6, 8] sts, sc in each of next 1 [2, 2] st(s), 2 sc in next st, sc in last st, join in beg sc. *(36 [40, 44] sts)*

Rnd 4: Ch 2 *(see Pattern Notes)*, working in **back lp** *(see Stitch Guide)*, dc in each st around, join in first dc. *(36 [40, 44] dc)*

Rnd 5: Ch 2 *(see Pattern Notes)*, hdc in each of next 9 [11, 13] sts, [hdc in next st, **hdc dec** *(see Stitch Guide)* in next 2 sts] 6 times, hdc in each of next 9 [11, 13] sts, join in beg hdc. *(30 [34, 38] sts)*

Rnd 6: Ch 2, hdc in each of next 9 [11, 13] sts, [hdc dec in next 2 sts] 6 times, hdc in each of next 9 [11, 13] sts, join in beg hdc. *(24 [28, 32] sts)*

Rnd 7: Ch 2, hdc in each of next 8 [10, 12] sts, [hdc dec in next 2 sts] 4 times, hdc in each of next 8 [10, 12] sts, join in beg hdc. *(20 [24, 28] sts)*

Rnd 8: Ch 2, hdc in each of next 7 [9, 11] sts, hdc dec in next 2 sts, hdc in each of next 2 sts, hdc dec in next 2 sts, hdc in each of next 7 [9, 11] sts, join in beg hdc. *(18 [22, 26] sts)*

Rnd 9: Ch 3 *(see Pattern Notes)*, dc in same st as beg ch-3, sk next st, [2 dc in next st, sk next st] 8 [10, 12] times, join in beg ch-3. *(9 [11, 13] 2-dc groups)*

Rnd 10: Sl st in sp between beg ch-3 and next dc, ch 3, dc in same sp, [2 dc in sp between next 2 dc] around, join in beg ch-3.

Rnds 11–13: Rep rnd 10. At the end of rnd 13, fasten off. ●

Little Man

Continued from page 15

Rnd 5: Ch 1, sc in each of next 12 [14, 16] sts, sc dec in next 2 sts, sc in each of next 4 sts, sc dec in next 2 sts, sc in each of next 12 [14, 16] sts, join in beg sc. *(30 [34, 38] sts)*

Rnd 6: Ch 1, sc in each of next 10 [12, 14] sts, working in back lps, [sc dec in next 2 sc] 5 times, working in both lps, sc in each of next 10 [12, 14] sts, join in beg sc. *(25 [29, 33] sts)*

Rnd 7: Ch 2 *(see Pattern Notes)*, dc in each of next 3 sts, hdc in next hdc, sc in each of next 6 [8, 10] sts, **dc dec** *(see Stitch Guide)* in next 2 sts, dc in next st, dc dec in next 2 sts, sc in each of next 6 [8, 10] sts, hdc in next st, dc in each of next 3 sts, join in first dc. Fasten off. *(23 [27, 31] sts)*

Strap

Rnd 1: Ch 10, sc in 2nd ch from hook, sc in each of next 7 chs, 3 sc in last ch, working on opposite side of foundation ch, sc in each of next 7 chs, 2 sc in last ch, join in beg sc. *(20 sc)*

Rnd 2: Ch 1, 2 sc in first st, sc in each of next 7 sts, 2 sc in next st, sc in next st, 2 sc in next st, sc in each of next 7 sts, 2 sc in next st, sc in next st, join in beg sc. Fasten off. *(24 sc)* ●

STITCH GUIDE

Need help? ▶ **StitchGuide.com** • ILLUSTRATED GUIDES • HOW-TO VIDEOS

STITCH ABBREVIATIONS

beg .... begin/begins/beginning
bpdc .... back post double crochet
bpsc .... back post single crochet
bptr .... back post treble crochet
CC .... contrasting color
ch(s) .... chain(s)
ch- .... refers to chain or space
          previously made (i.e., ch-1 space)
ch sp(s) .... chain space(s)
cl(s) .... cluster(s)
cm .... centimeter(s)
dc .... double crochet (singular/plural)
dc dec .... double crochet 2 or more
          stitches together, as indicated
dec .... decrease/decreases/decreasing
dtr .... double treble crochet
ext .... extended
fpdc .... front post double crochet
fpsc .... front post single crochet
fptr .... front post treble crochet
g .... gram(s)
hdc .... half double crochet
hdc dec .... half double crochet 2 or more
          stitches together, as indicated
inc .... increase/increases/increasing
lp(s) .... loop(s)
MC .... main color
mm .... millimeter(s)
oz .... ounce(s)
pc .... popcorn(s)
rem .... remain/remains/remaining
rep(s) .... repeat(s)
rnd(s) .... round(s)
RS .... right side
sc .... single crochet (singular/plural)
sc dec .... single crochet 2 or more
          stitches together, as indicated
sk .... skip/skipped/skipping
sl st(s) .... slip stitch(es)
sp(s) .... space(s)/spaced
st(s) .... stitch(es)
tog .... together
tr .... treble crochet
trtr .... triple treble
WS .... wrong side
yd(s) .... yard(s)
yo .... yarn over

YARN CONVERSION

OUNCES TO GRAMS		GRAMS TO OUNCES	
1	28.4	25	⅞
2	56.7	40	1⅔
3	85.0	50	1¾
4	113.4	100	3½

UNITED STATES		UNITED KINGDOM
sl st (slip stitch)	=	sc (single crochet)
sc (single crochet)	=	dc (double crochet)
hdc (half double crochet)	=	htr (half treble crochet)
dc (double crochet)	=	tr (treble crochet)
tr (treble crochet)	=	dtr (double treble crochet)
dtr (double treble crochet)	=	ttr (triple treble crochet)
skip	=	miss

Single crochet decrease (sc dec):
(Insert hook, yo, draw lp through) in each of the sts indicated, yo, draw through all lps on hook.

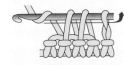

Example of 2-sc dec

Half double crochet decrease (hdc dec):
(Yo, insert hook, yo, draw lp through) in each of the sts indicated, yo, draw through all lps on hook.

Example of 2-hdc dec

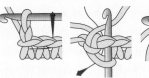

Reverse single crochet (reverse sc):
Ch 1, sk first st, working from left to right, insert hook in next st from front to back, draw up lp on hook, yo and draw through both lps on hook.

Chain (ch):
Yo, pull through lp on hook.

Single crochet (sc):
Insert hook in st, yo, pull through st, yo, pull through both lps on hook.

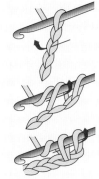

Double crochet (dc):
Yo, insert hook in st, yo, pull through st, [yo, pull through 2 lps] twice.

Double crochet decrease (dc dec):
(Yo, insert hook, yo, draw lp through, yo, draw through 2 lps on hook) in each of the sts indicated, yo, draw through all lps on hook.

Example of 2-dc dec

Front loop (front lp) Back loop (back lp)

Front Loop   Back Loop

Front post stitch (fp): Back post stitch (bp):
When working post st, insert hook from right to left around post of st on previous row.

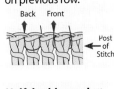

Back   Front
                Post
                of
                Stitch

Half double crochet (hdc):
Yo, insert hook in st, yo, pull through st, yo, pull through all 3 lps on hook.

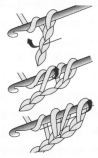

Double treble crochet (dtr):
Yo 3 times, insert hook in st, yo, pull through st, [yo, pull through 2 lps] 4 times.

Treble crochet decrease (tr dec):
Holding back last lp of each st, tr in each of the sts indicated, yo, pull through all lps on hook.

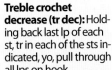

Example of 2-tr dec

Slip stitch (sl st):
Insert hook in st, pull through both lps on hook.

Chain color change (ch color change)
Yo with new color, draw through last lp on hook.

Double crochet color change (dc color change)
Drop first color, yo with new color, draw through last 2 lps of st.

Treble crochet (tr):
Yo twice, insert hook in st, yo, pull through st, [yo, pull through 2 lps] 3 times.

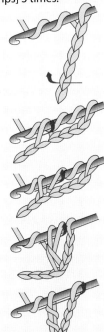

Metric Conversion Charts

METRIC CONVERSIONS

yards	x	.9144	=	metres (m)
yards	x	91.44	=	centimetres (cm)
inches	x	2.54	=	centimetres (cm)
inches	x	25.40	=	millimetres (mm)
inches	x	.0254	=	metres (m)

centimetres	x	.3937	=	inches
metres	x	1.0936	=	yards

INCHES INTO MILLIMETRES & CENTIMETRES (Rounded off slightly)

inches	mm	cm	inches	cm	inches	cm	inches	cm
1/8	3	0.3	5	12.5	21	53.5	38	96.5
1/4	6	0.6	5 1/2	14	22	56	39	99
3/8	10	1	6	15	23	58.5	40	101.5
1/2	13	1.3	7	18	24	61	41	104
5/8	15	1.5	8	20.5	25	63.5	42	106.5
3/4	20	2	9	23	26	66	43	109
7/8	22	2.2	10	25.5	27	68.5	44	112
1	25	2.5	11	28	28	71	45	114.5
1 1/4	32	3.2	12	30.5	29	73.5	46	117
1 1/2	38	3.8	13	33	30	76	47	119.5
1 3/4	45	4.5	14	35.5	31	79	48	122
2	50	5	15	38	32	81.5	49	124.5
2 1/2	65	6.5	16	40.5	33	84	50	127
3	75	7.5	17	43	34	86.5		
3 1/2	90	9	18	46	35	89		
4	100	10	19	48.5	36	91.5		
4 1/2	115	11.5	20	51	37	94		

KNITTING NEEDLES CONVERSION CHART

Canada/U.S.	0	1	2	3	4	5	6	7	8	9	10	10½	11	13	15
Metric (mm)	2	2¼	2¾	3¼	3½	3¾	4	4½	5	5½	6	6½	8	9	10

CROCHET HOOKS CONVERSION CHART

Canada/U.S.	1/B	2/C	3/D	4/E	5/F	6/G	8/H	9/I	10/J	10½/K	N
Metric (mm)	2.25	2.75	3.25	3.5	3.75	4.25	5	5.5	6	6.5	9.0

Annie's

Sweet Shoes for Wee Ones is published by Annie's, 306 East Parr Road, Berne, IN 46711. Printed in USA. Copyright © 2015 Annie's. All rights reserved. This publication may not be reproduced in part or in whole without written permission from the publisher.

RETAIL STORES: If you would like to carry this publication or any other Annie's publication, visit AnniesWSL.com.

Every effort has been made to ensure that the instructions in this publication are complete and accurate. We cannot, however, take responsibility for human error, typographical mistakes or variations in individual work. Please visit AnniesCustomerService.com to check for pattern updates.

ISBN: 978-1-59012-275-4

1 2 3 4 5 6 7 8 9

The Story of Light

By Steve Vai

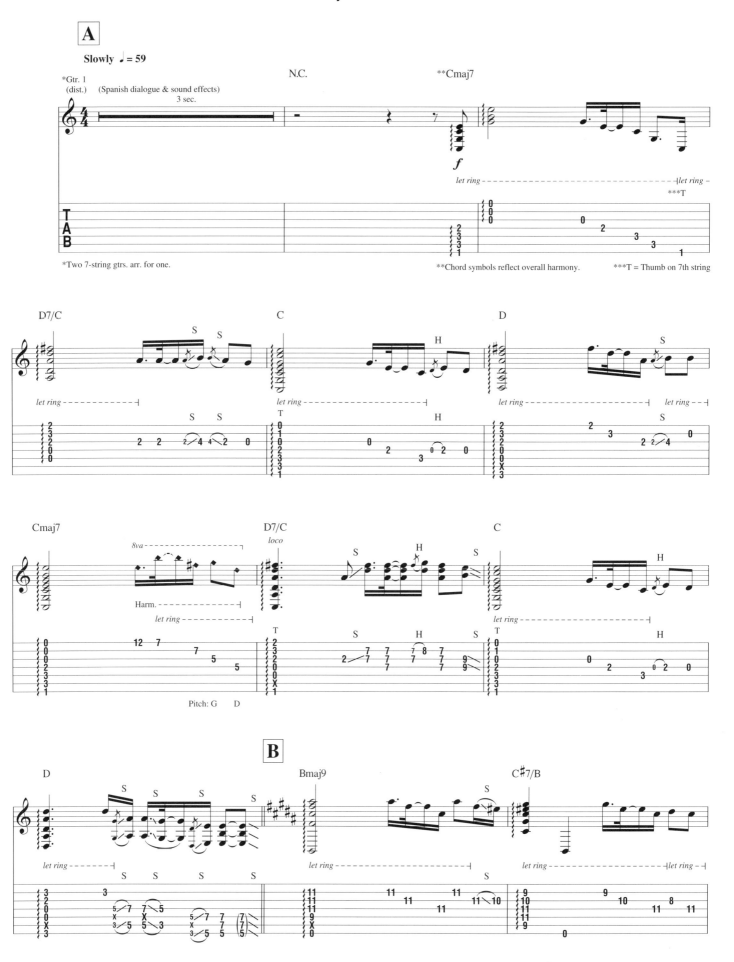

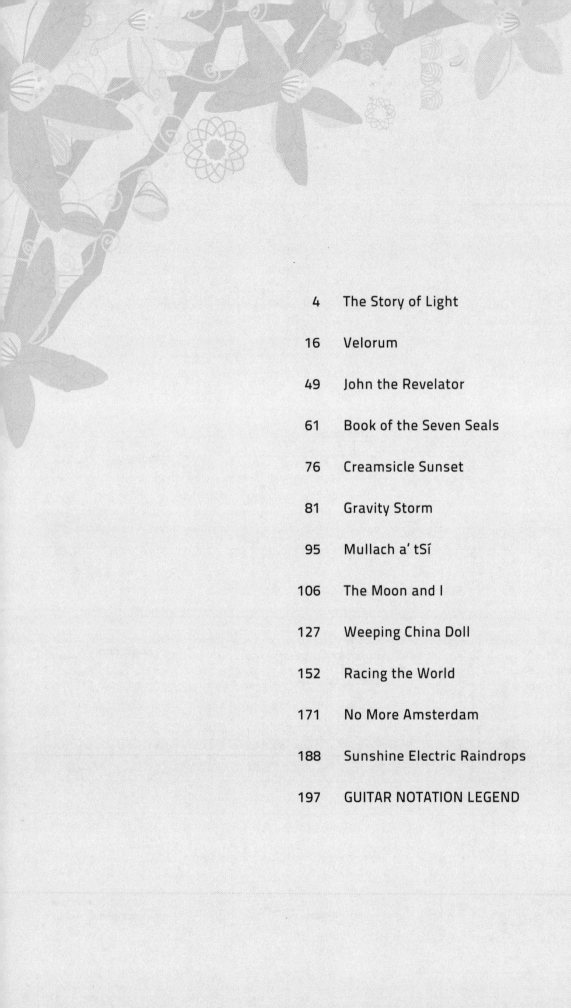

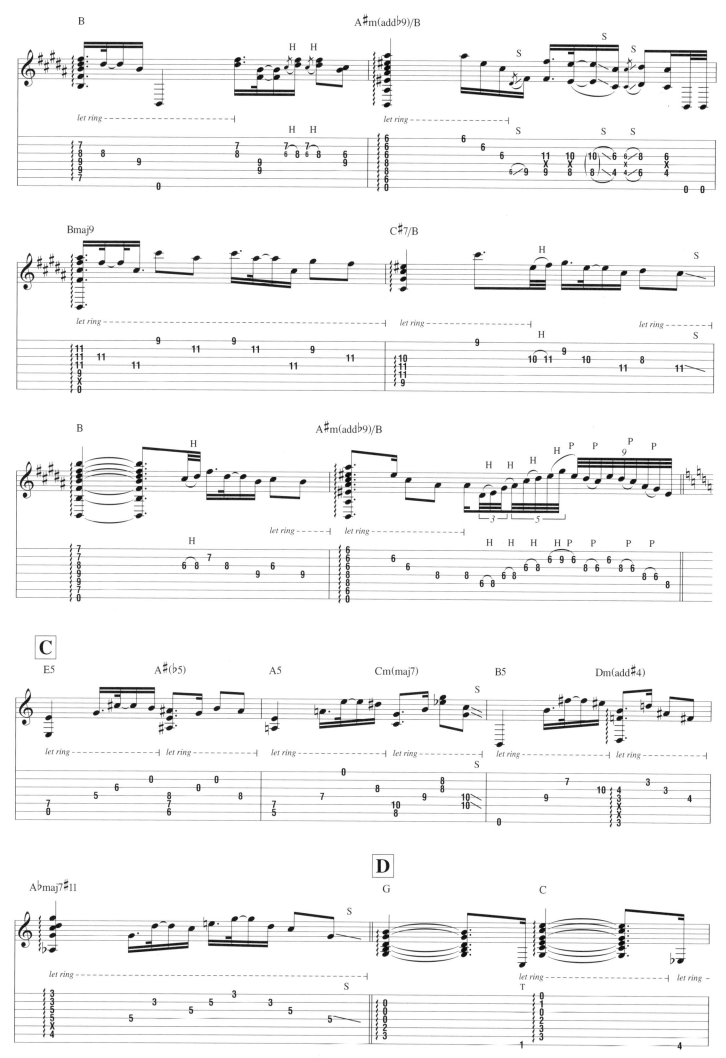

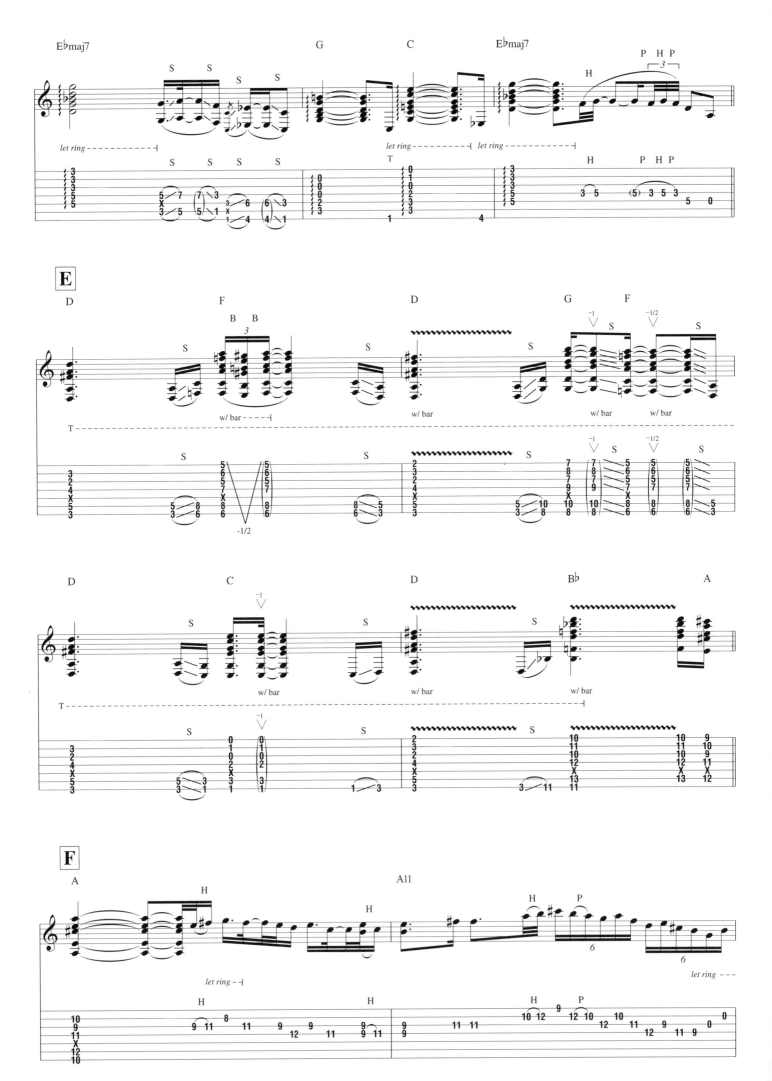

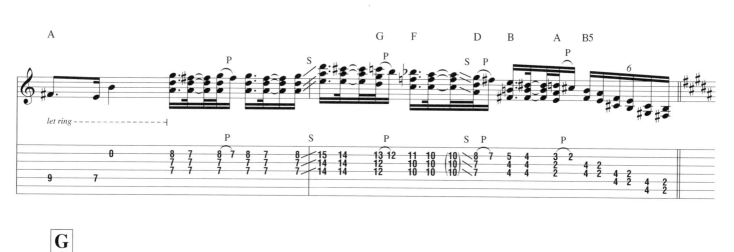

G

w/ Spanish dialog (next 5 meas.)

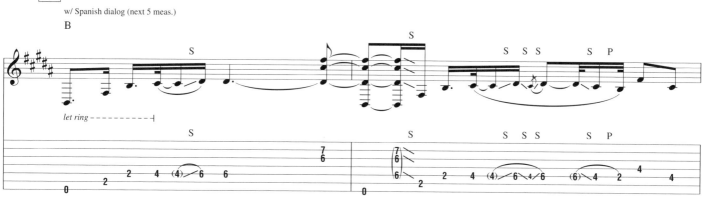

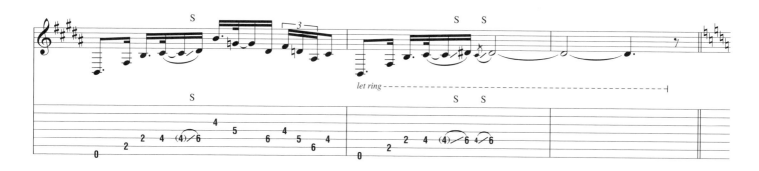

H

Cmaj7

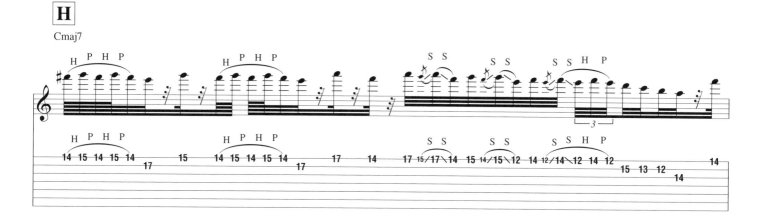

D7/C

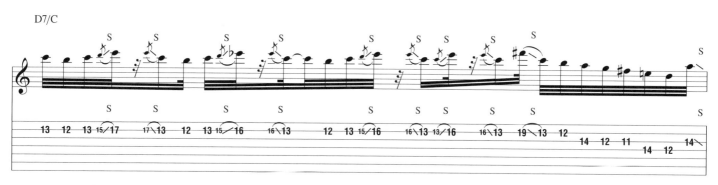

Cmaj7

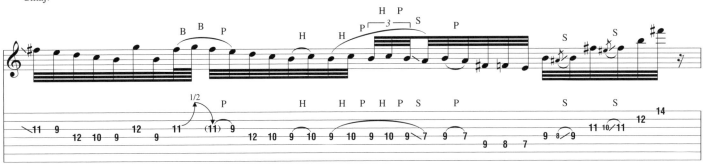

D

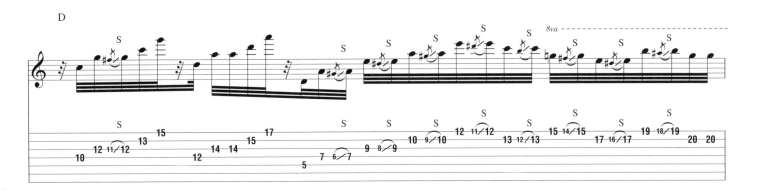

Cmaj7

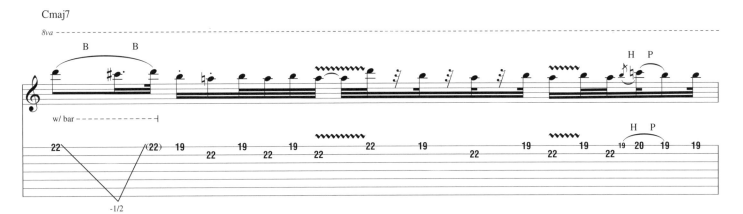

D

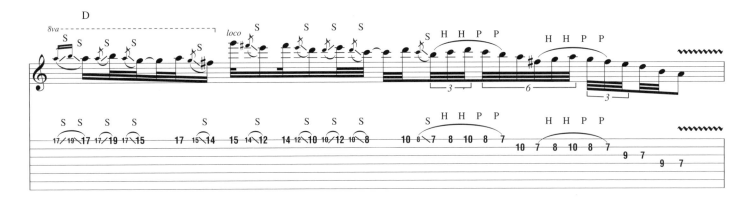

Cmaj7

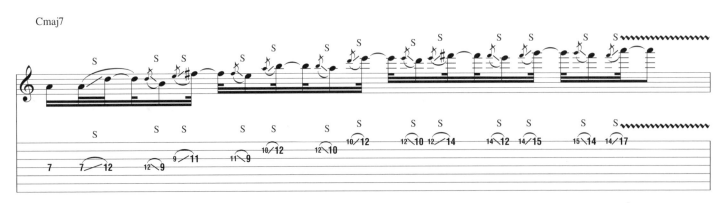

D

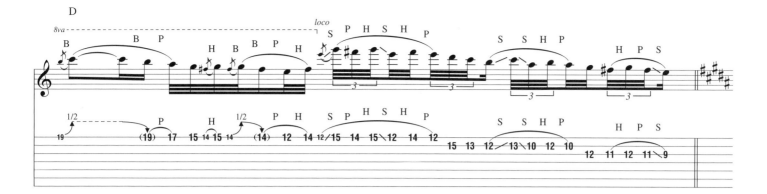

I

Double-time feel

Bmaj7

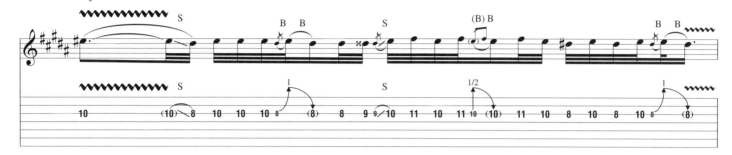

End double-time feel

C#7/B

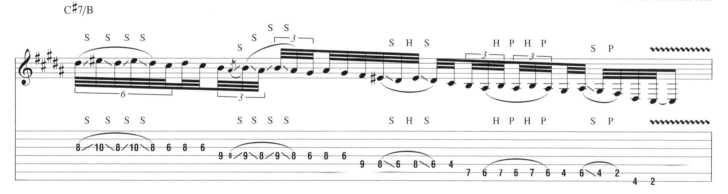

Bmaj7

C#7/B

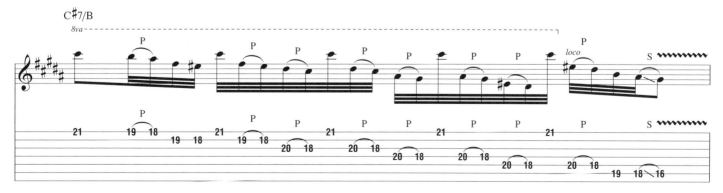

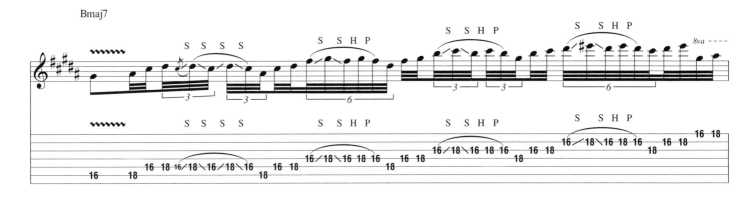

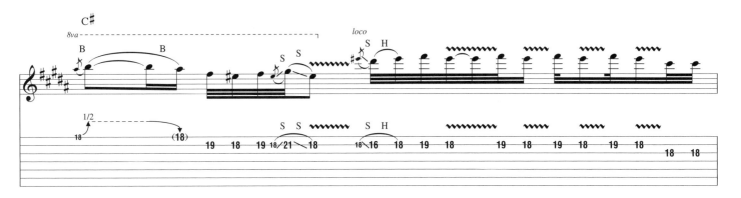

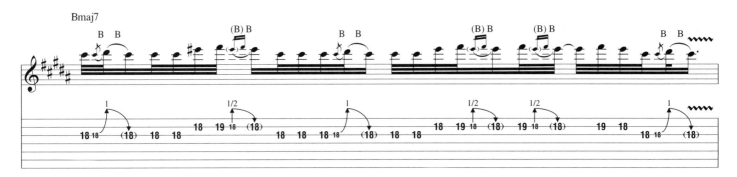

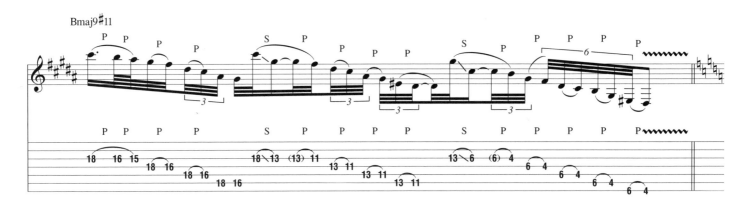

J

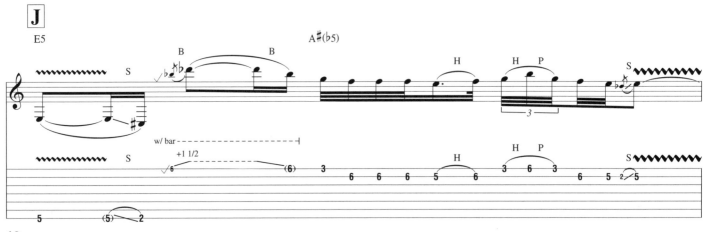

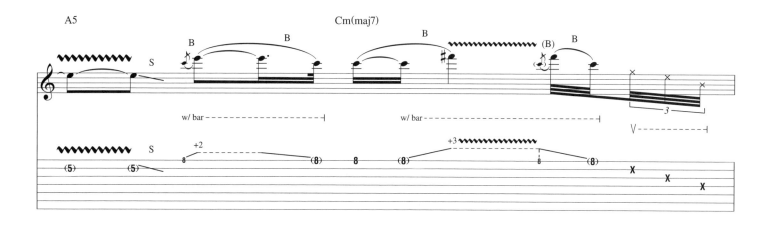

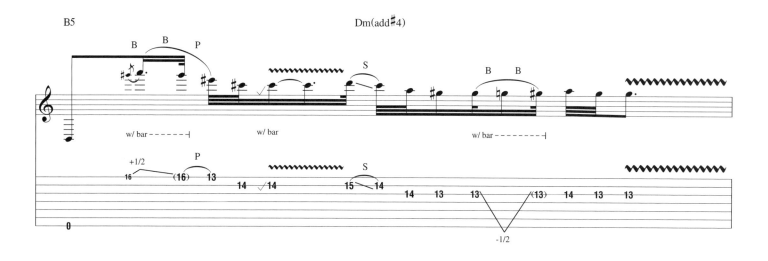

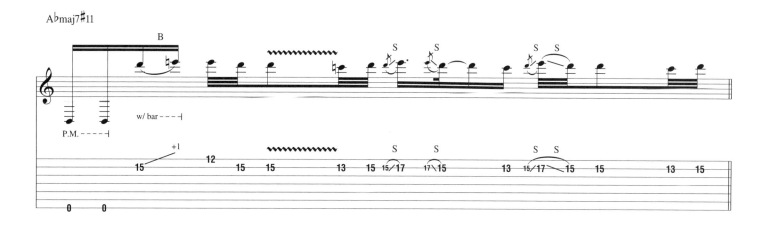

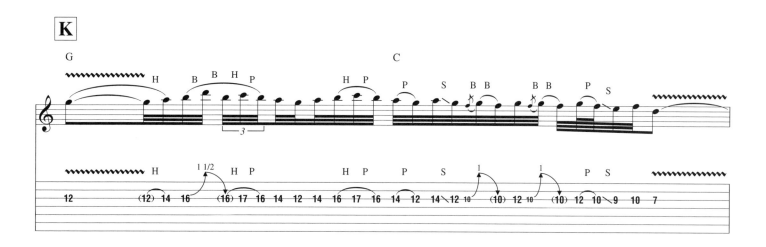

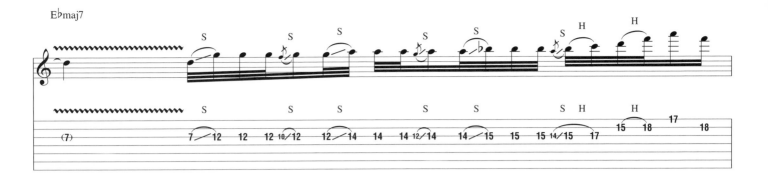

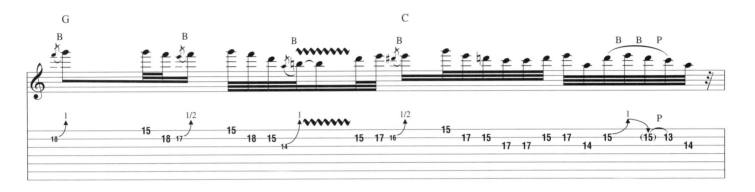

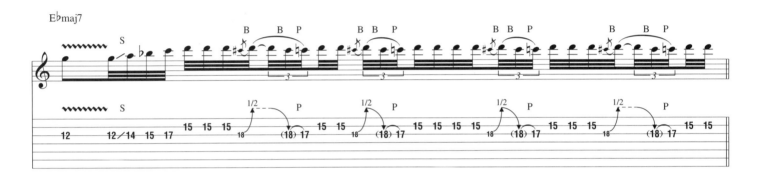

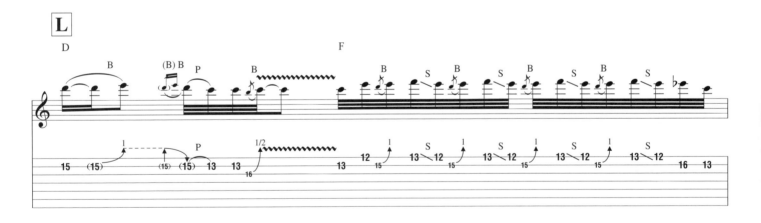

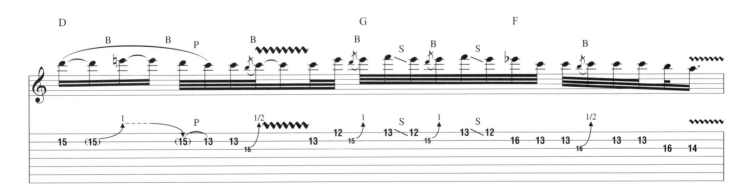

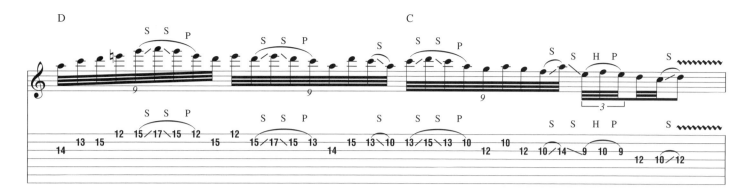

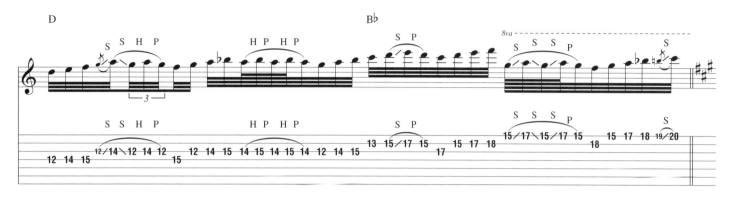

M

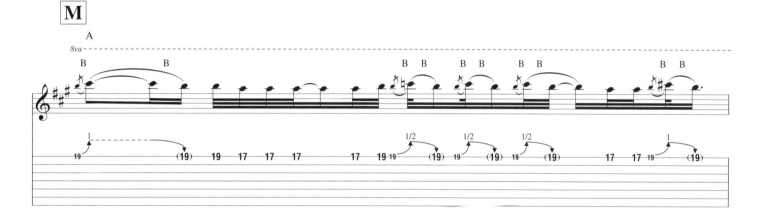

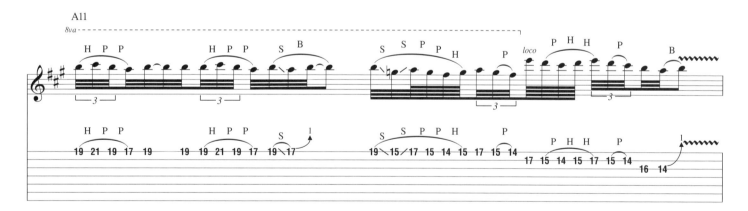

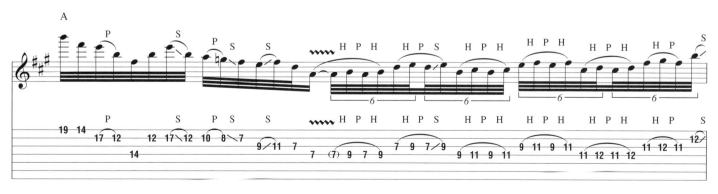

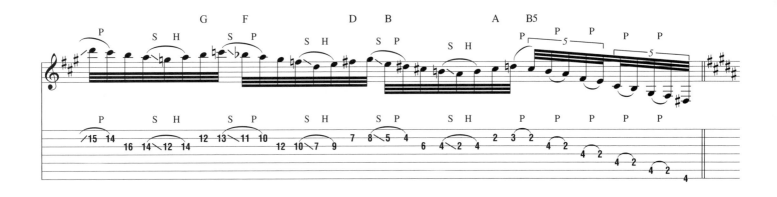

N

w/ Spanish dialog (till end)

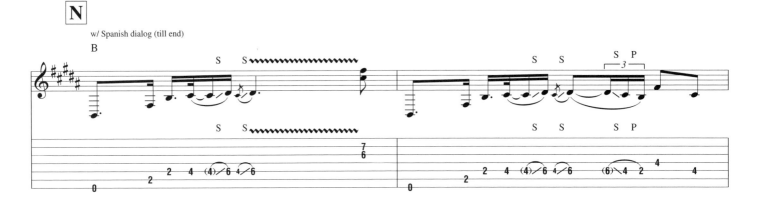

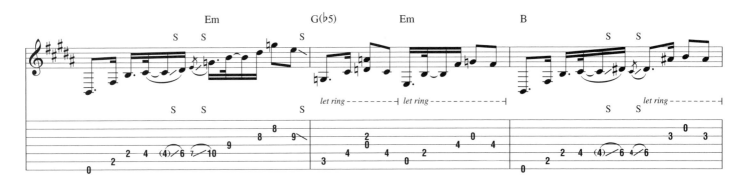

O

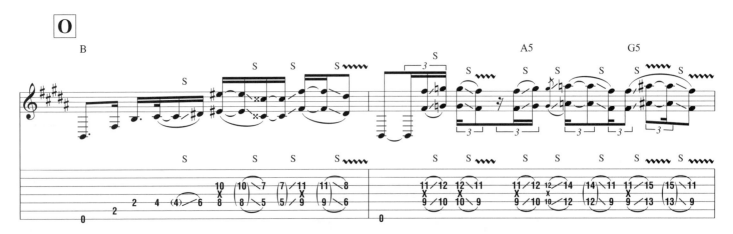

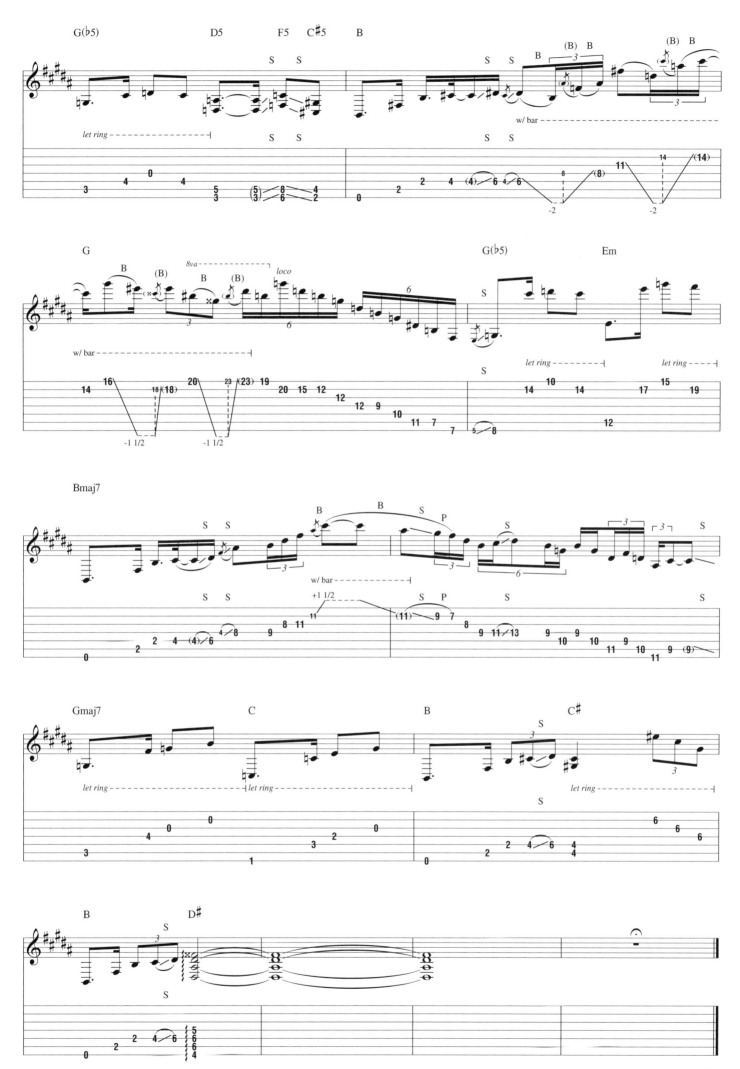

Velorum

By Steve Vai

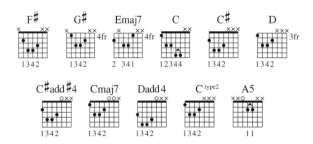

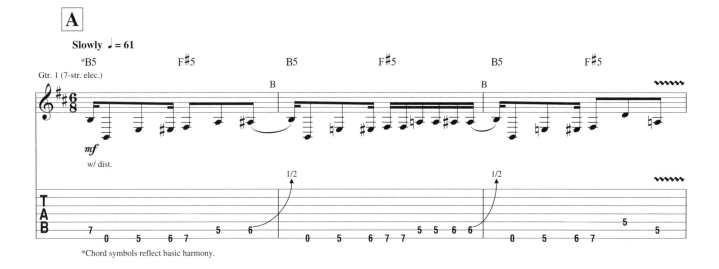

*Chord symbols reflect basic harmony.

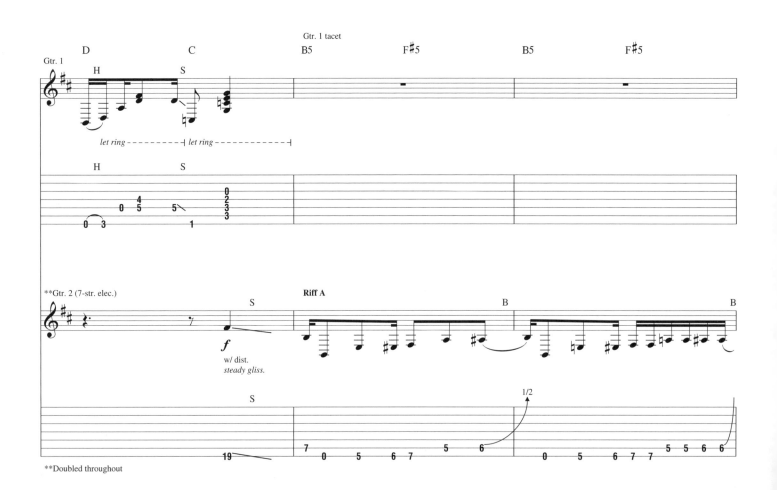

**Doubled throughout

*See top of first page of song for chord diagrams pertaining to rhythm slashes.

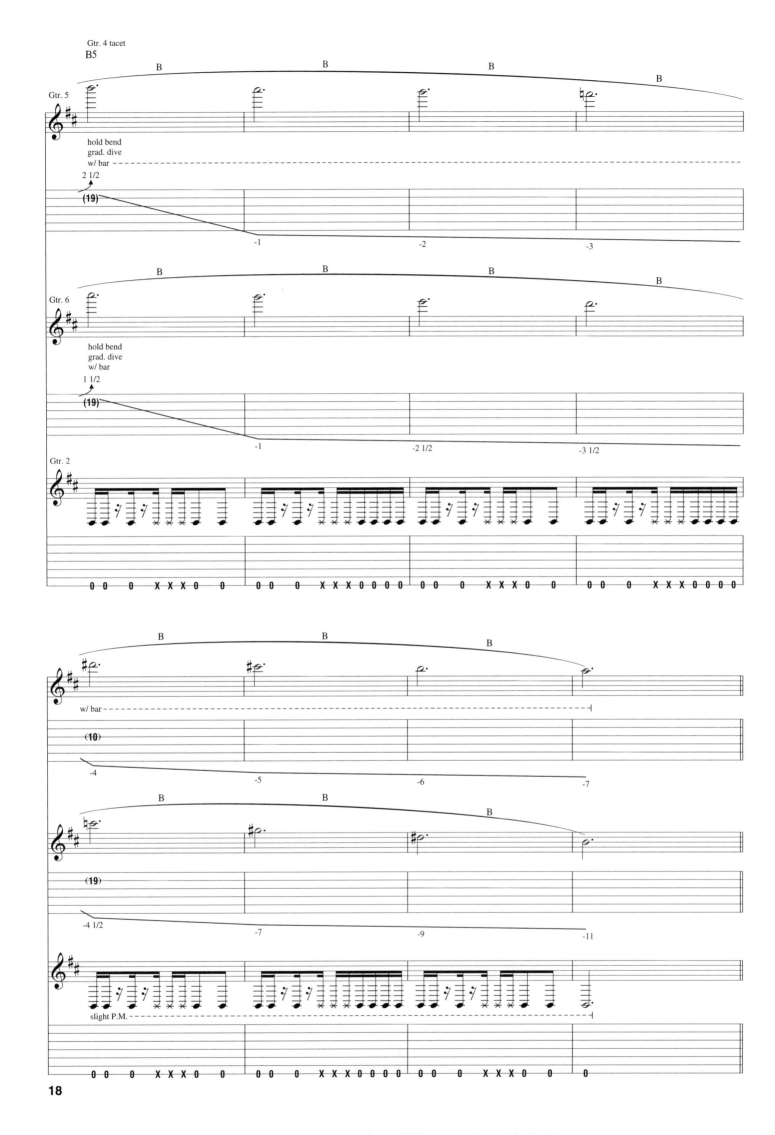

18

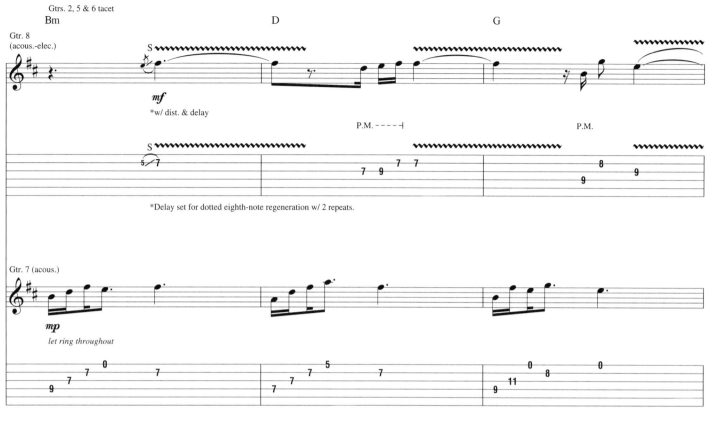

*Delay set for dotted eighth-note regeneration w/ 2 repeats.

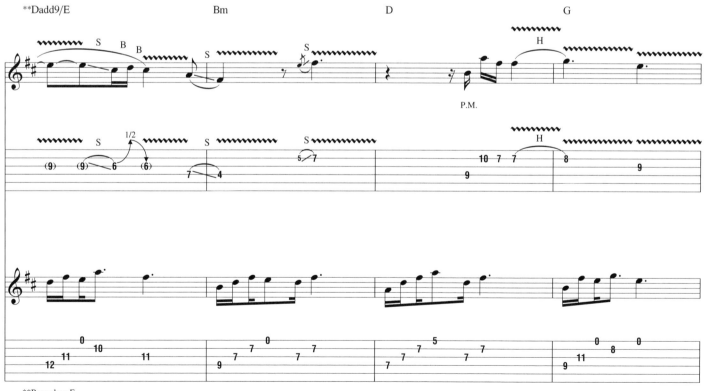

**Bass plays E.

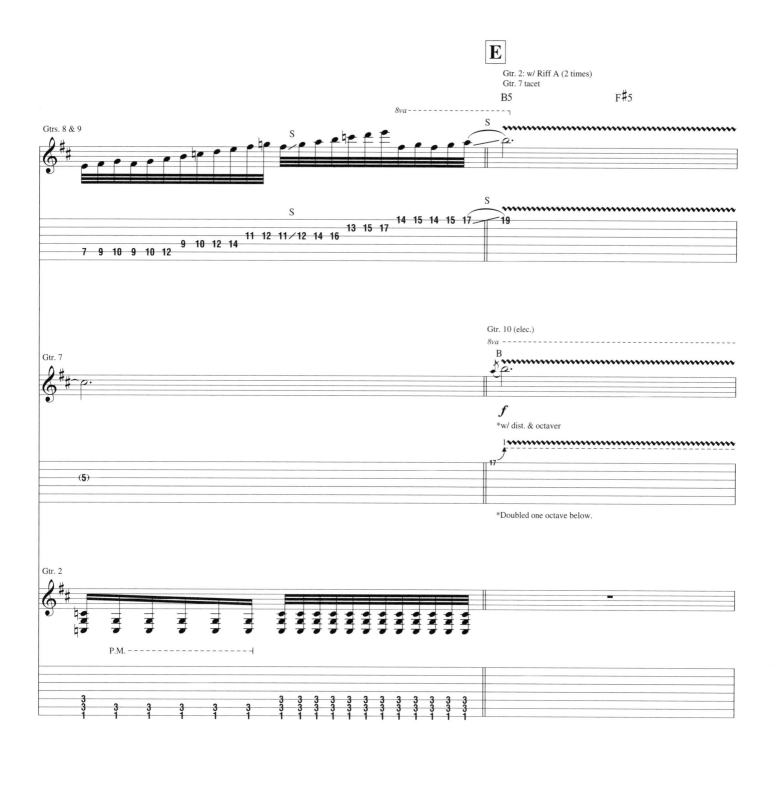

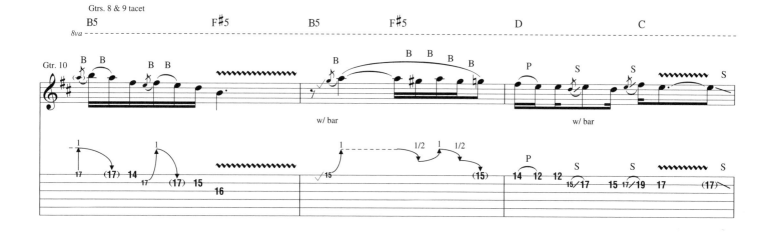

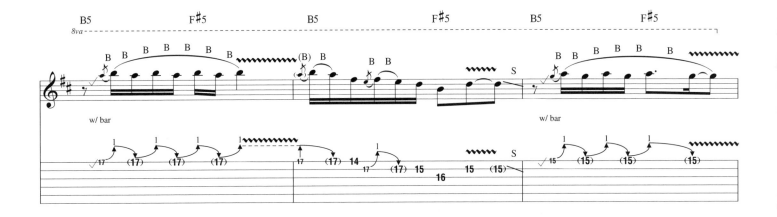

F

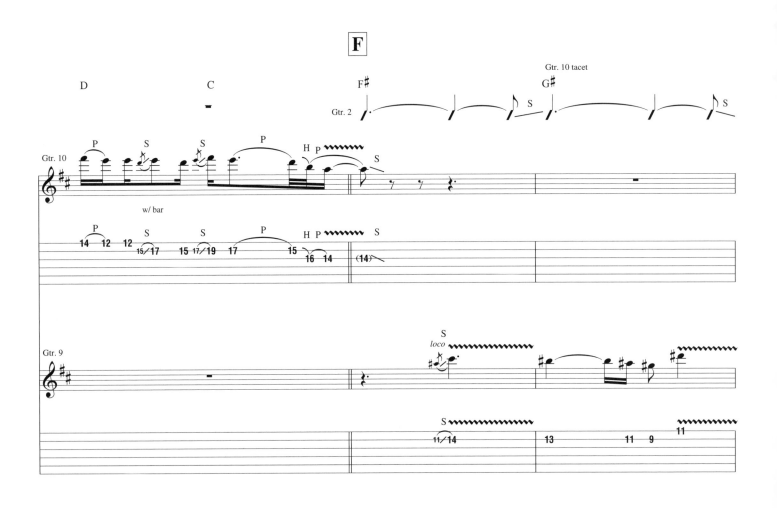

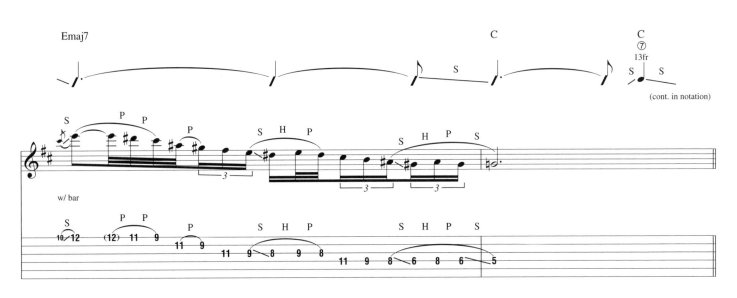

26

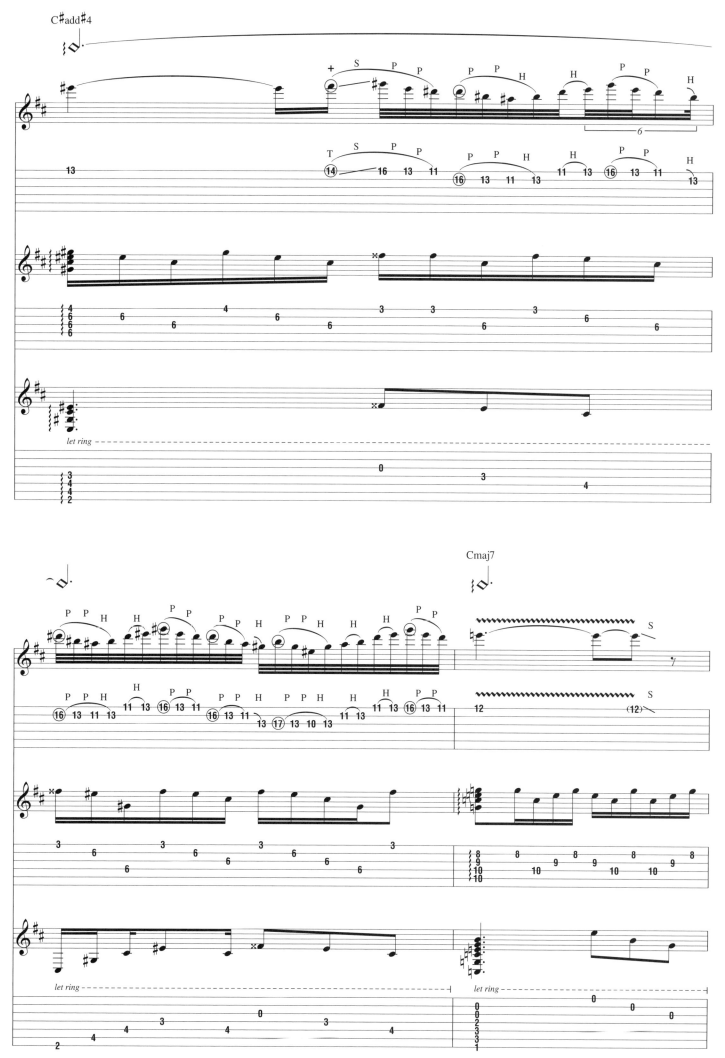

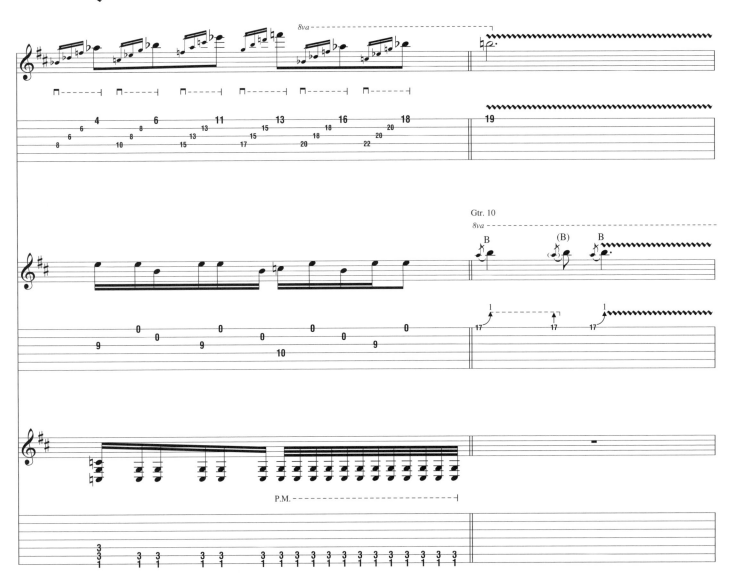

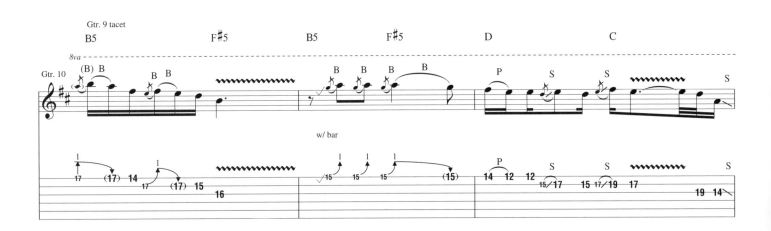

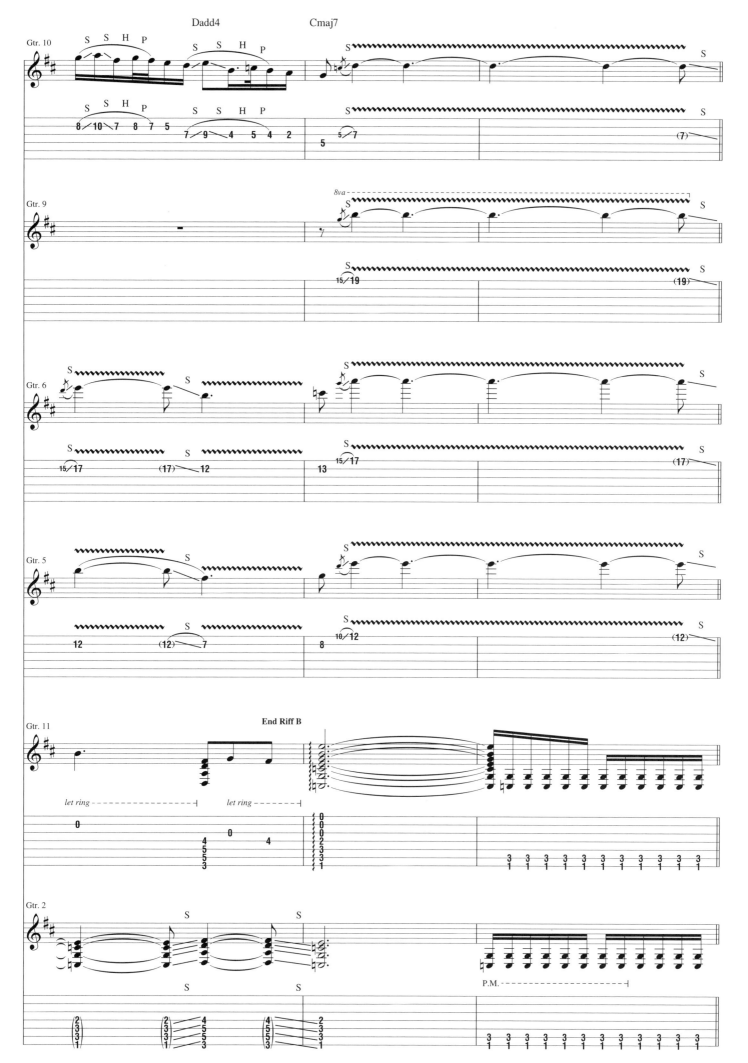

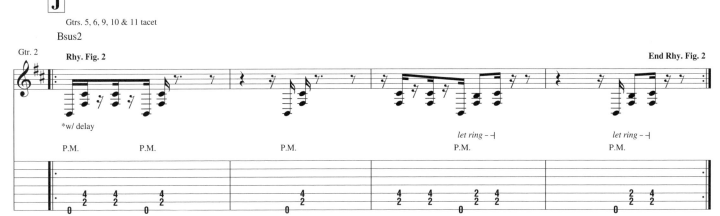

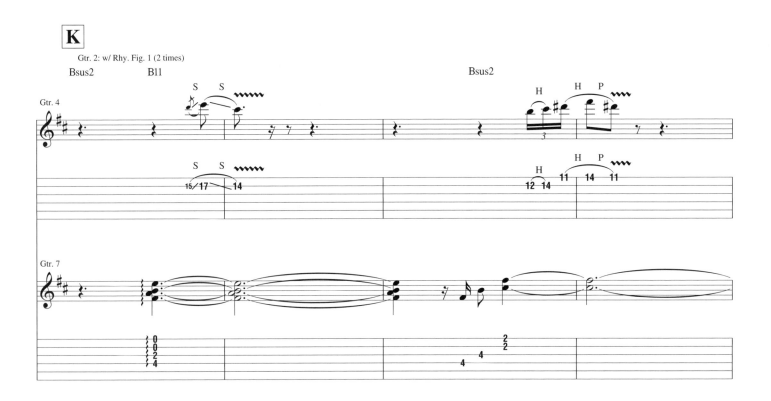

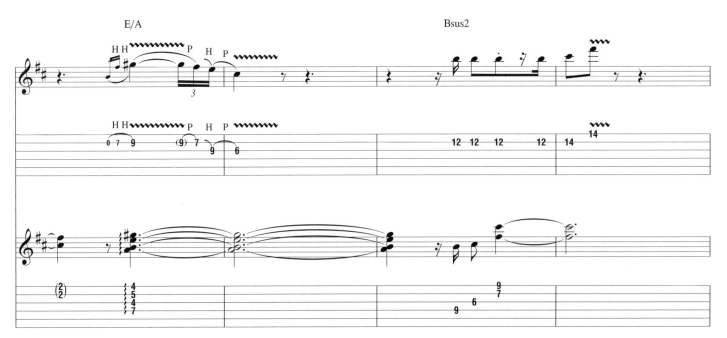

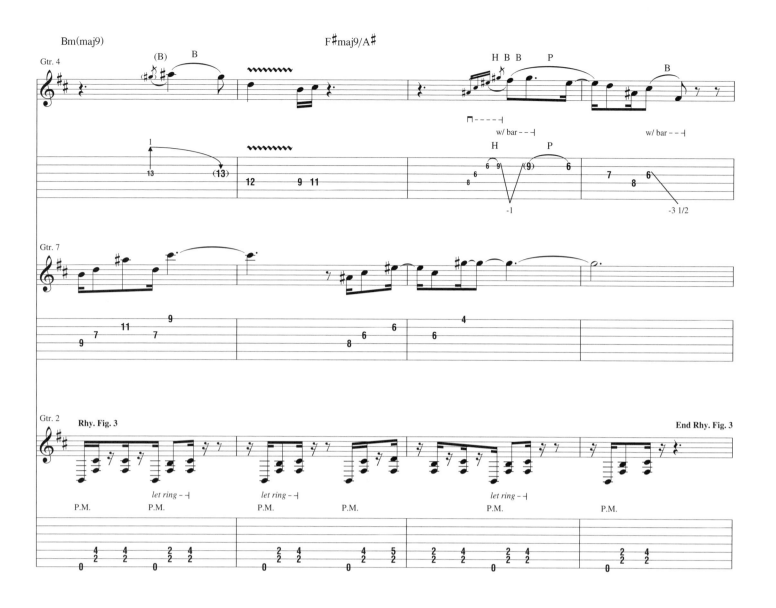

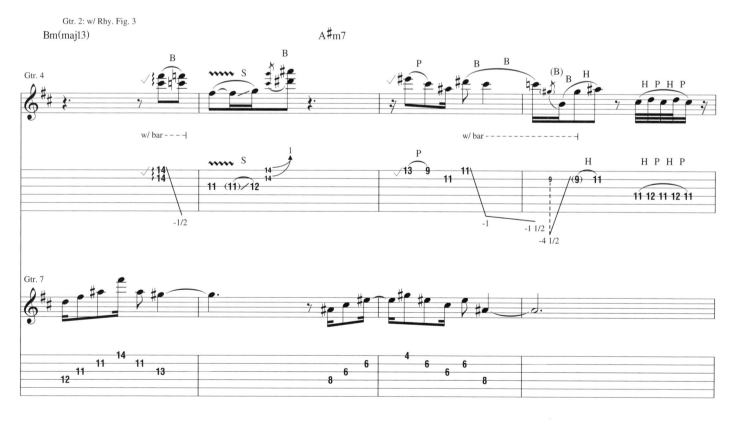

Bm(add4)

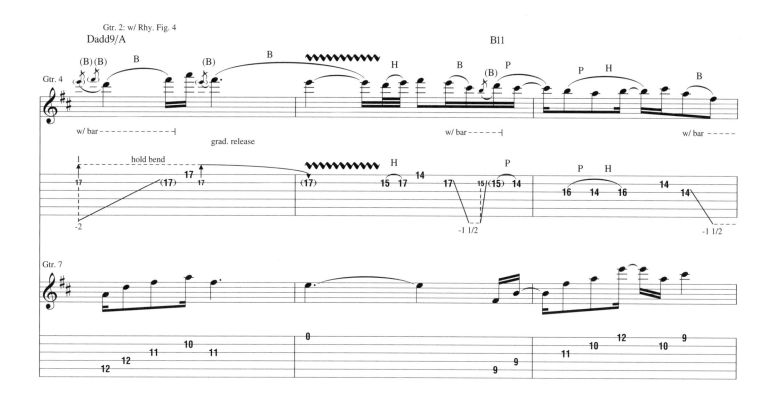

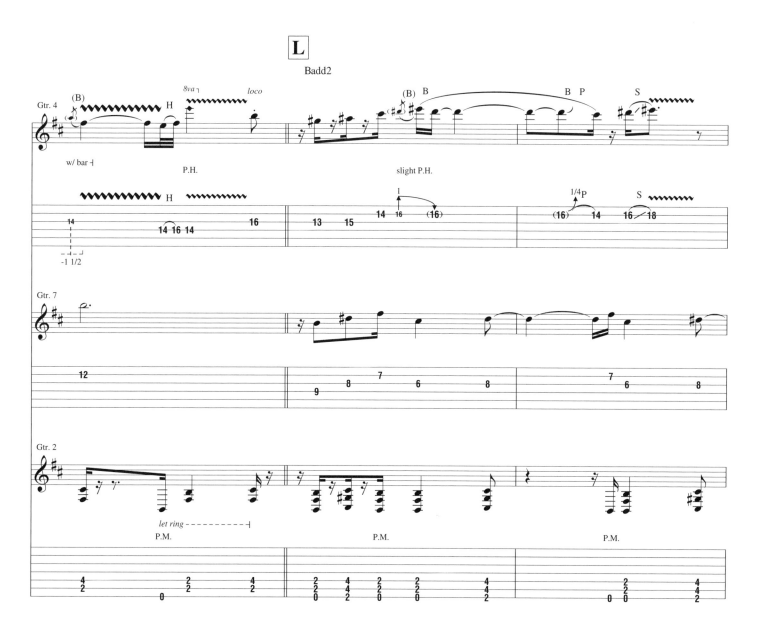

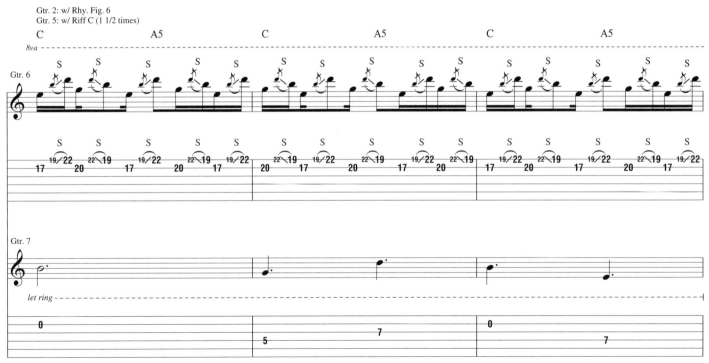

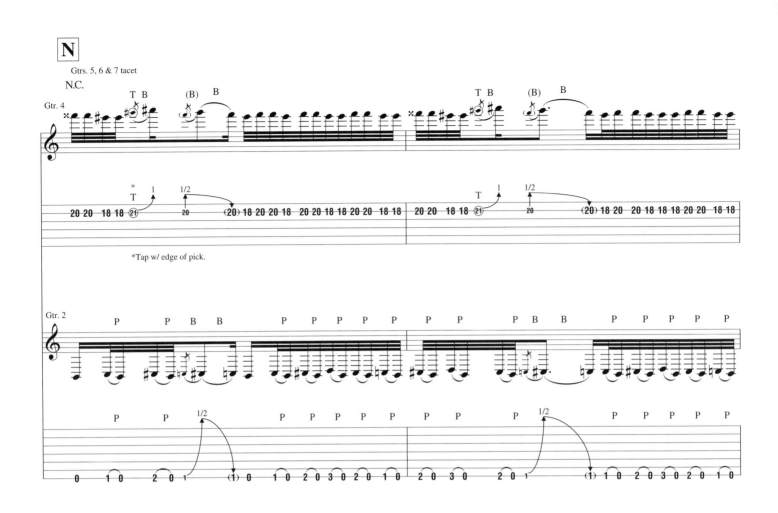

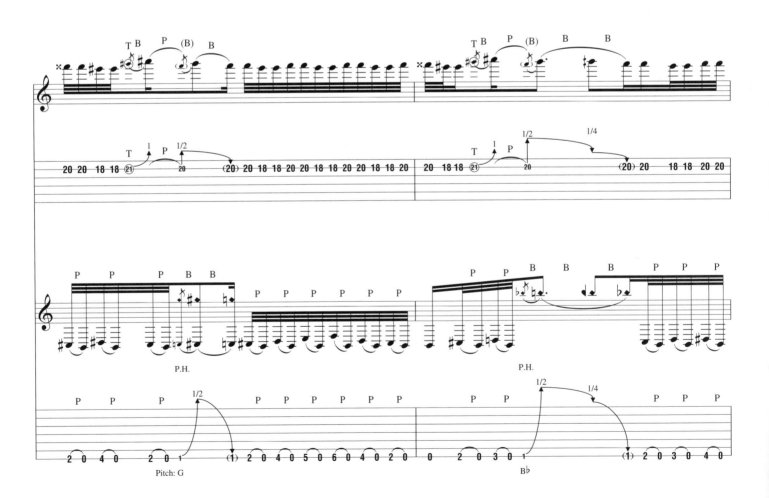

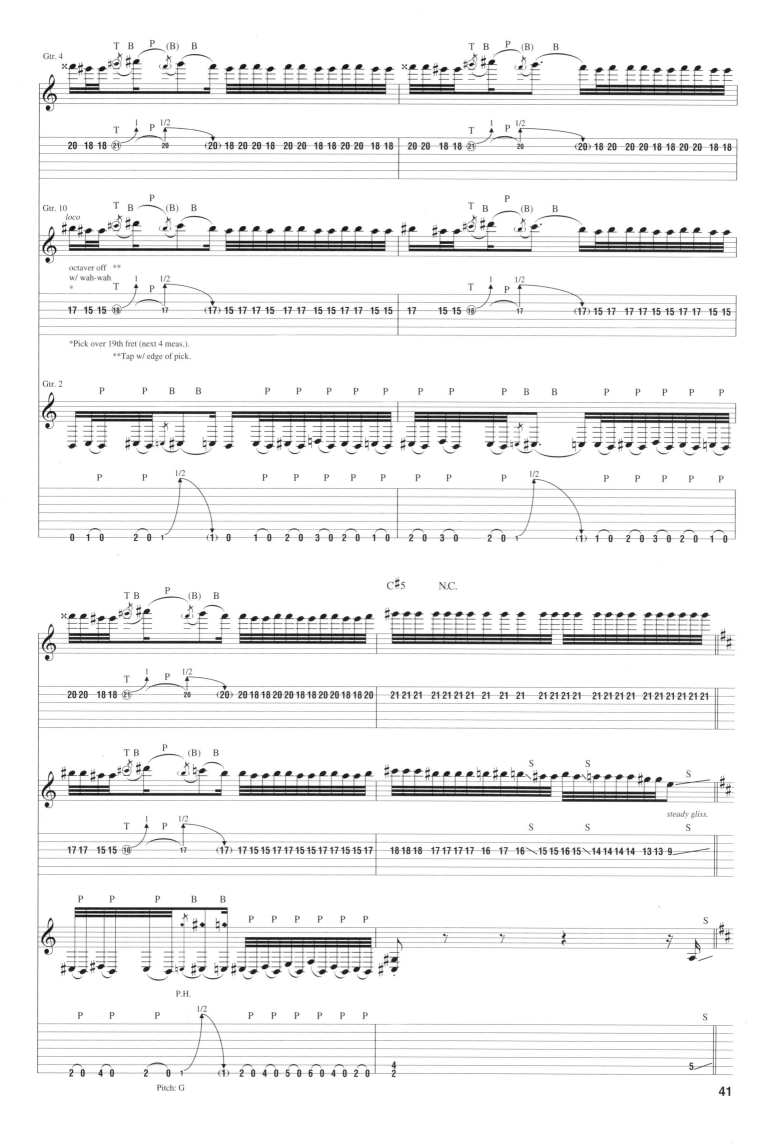

41

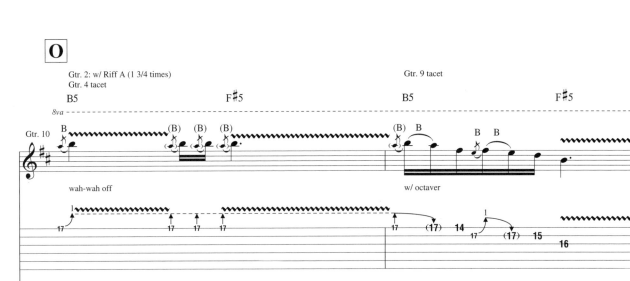

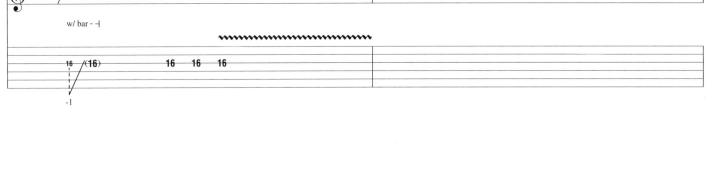

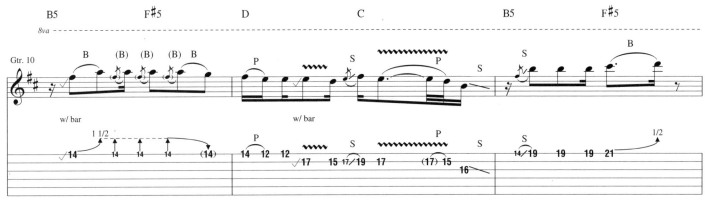

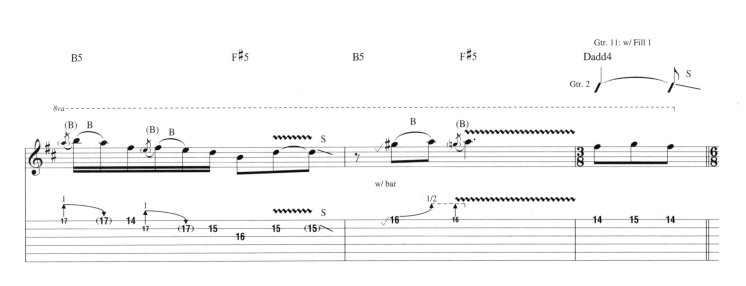

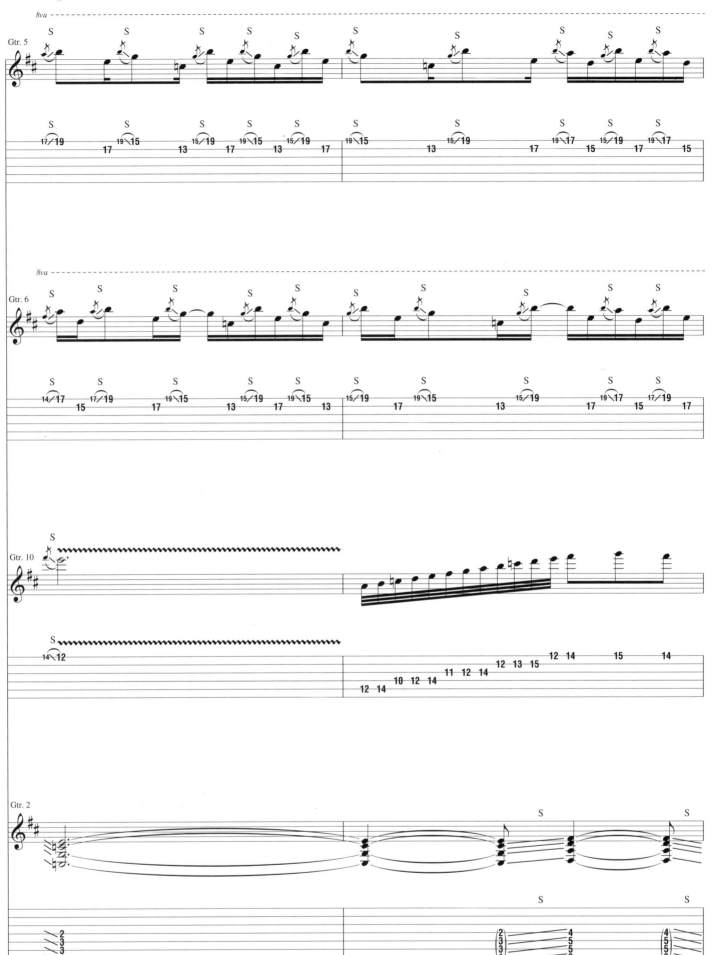

*Recorded at half speed.

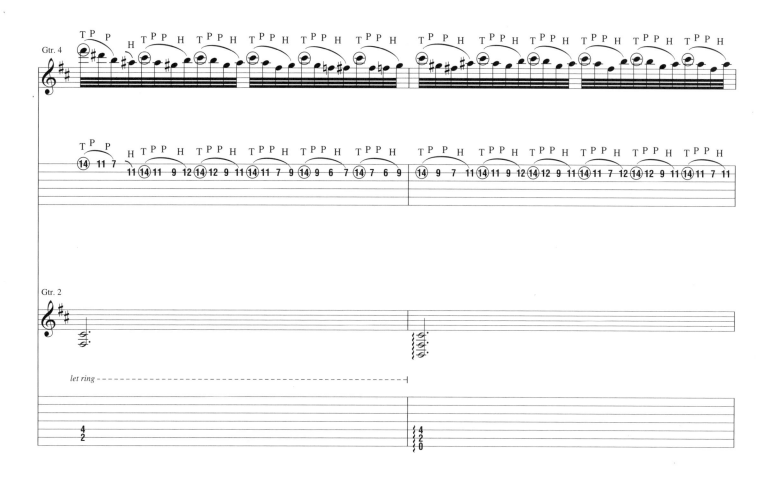

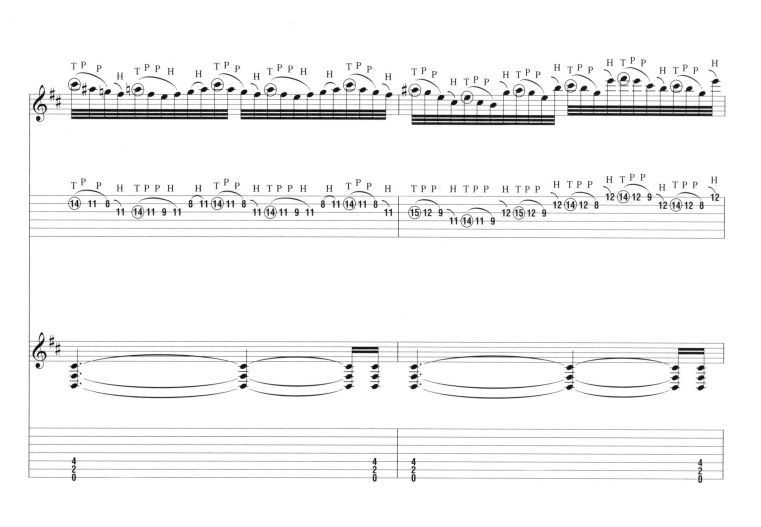

John the Revelator

Traditional Gospel
Arrangement by Steve Vai

Tune down 1 step:
(low to high) D-G-C-F-A-D

*Blind Willie Johnson sample

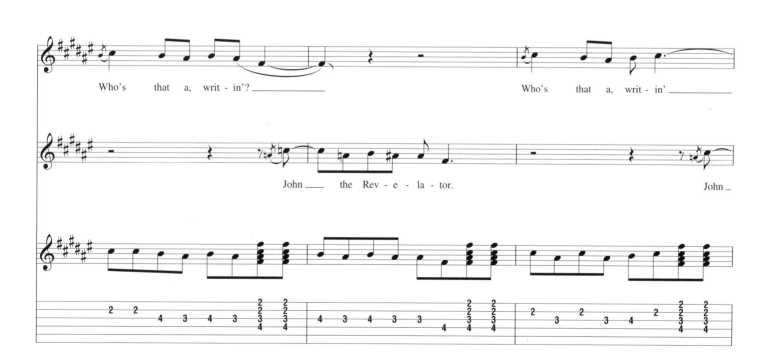

*Gtr. 1 part played as before.

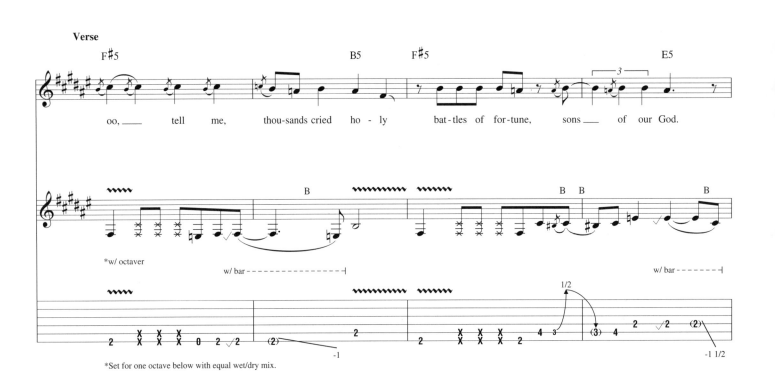

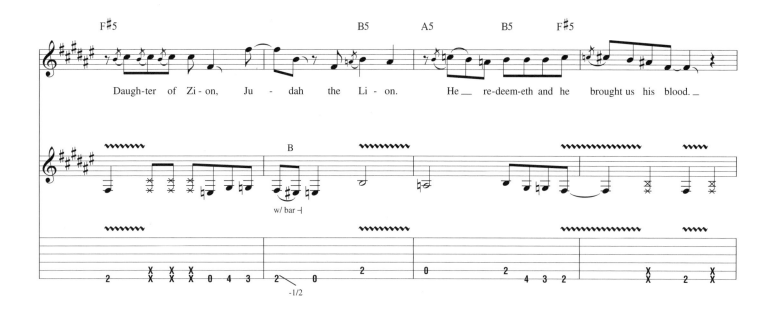

Daugh-ter of Zi - on, Ju - dah the Li - on. He — re-deem-eth and he brought us his blood. —

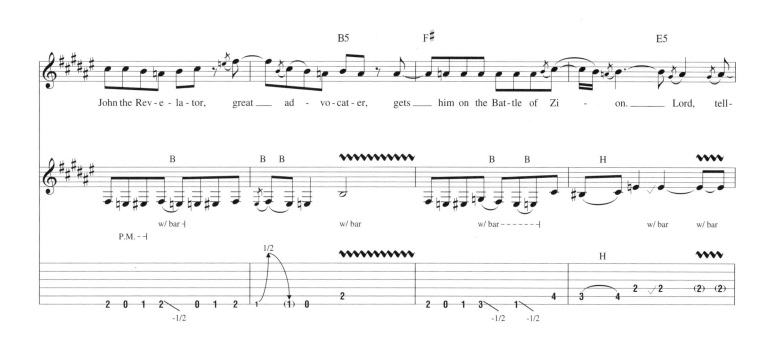

John the Rev - e - la - tor, great — ad - vo - cat - er, gets — him on the Bat - tle of Zi - on. Lord, tell-

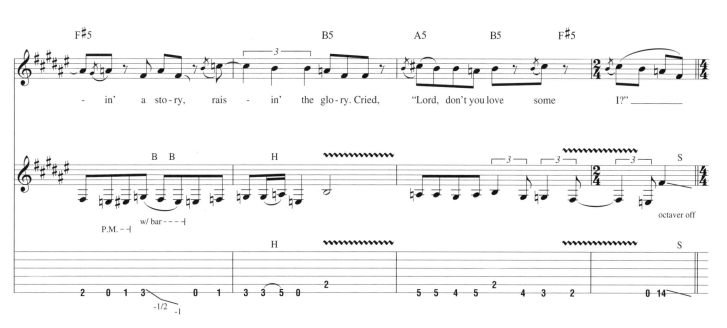

- in' a sto - ry, rais - in' the glo - ry. Cried, "Lord, don't you love some I?" ___

Chorus

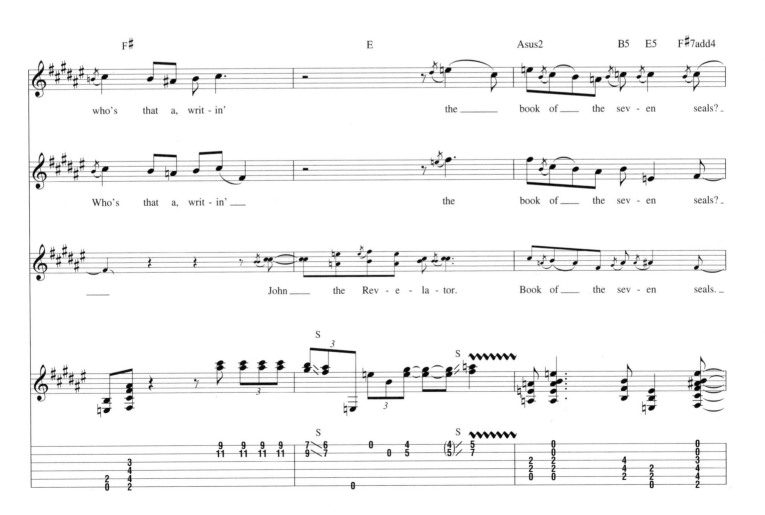

54

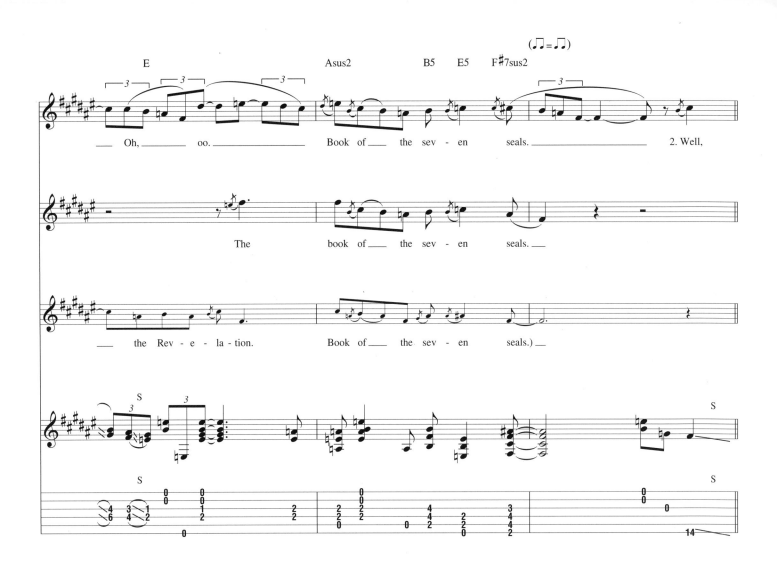

Oh, ___ oo. ___ Book of ___ the sev - en seals. ___ 2. Well,

The book of ___ the sev - en seals. ___

___ the Rev - e - la - tion. Book of ___ the sev - en seals.)

Verse

Mos - es to Mos - es, watch-in' the flock, __ yeah. Saw __ the bush where he had to stop. ___

*w/ octaver

w/ bar — — — — — — — — —|

*As before

-1

w/ bar — — — — — —|

-1 1/2

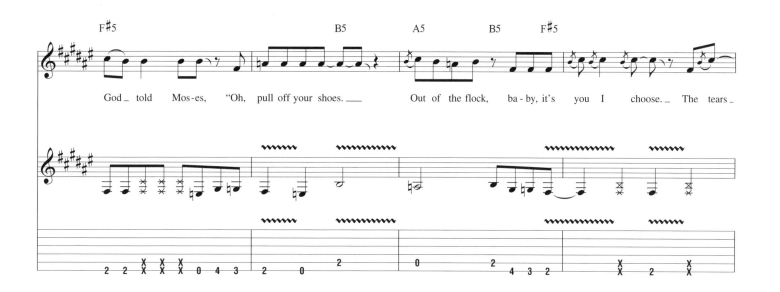

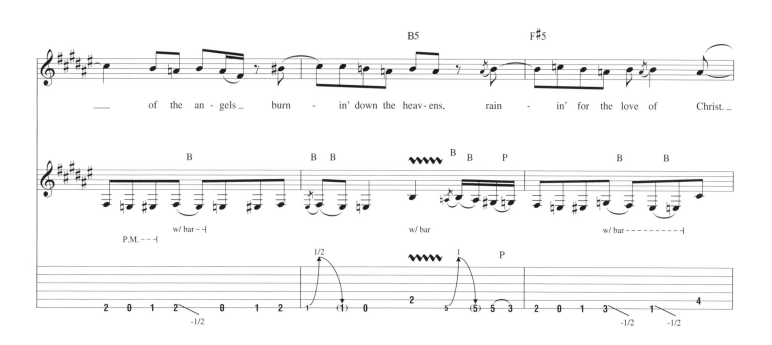

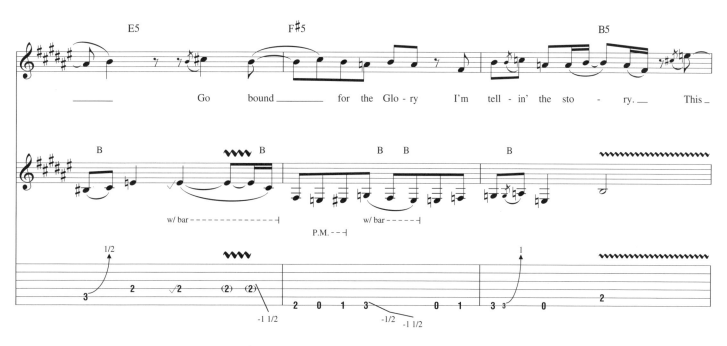

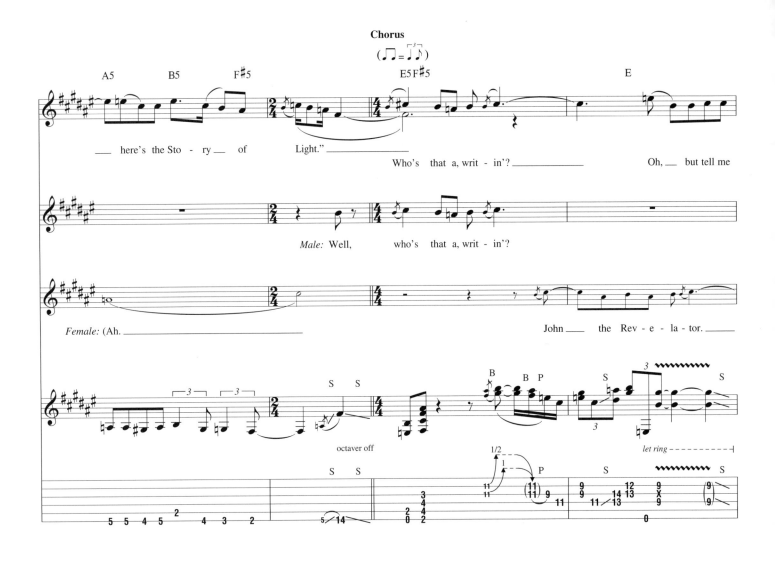

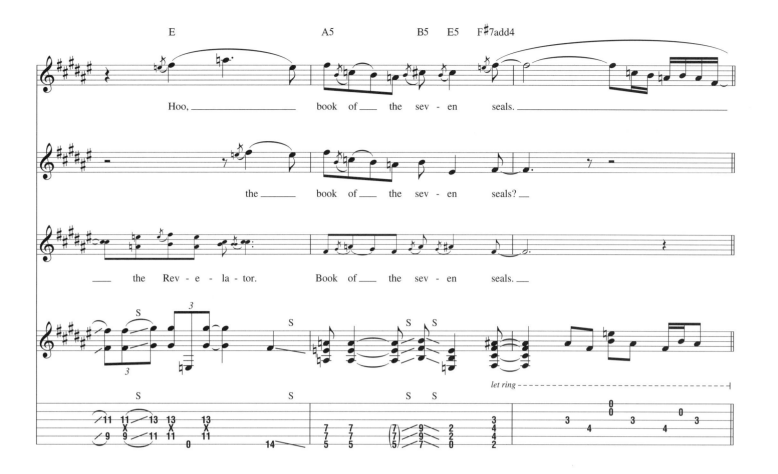

Hoo, _____ book of _____ the sev - en seals. _____

the _____ book of _____ the sev - en seals? _____

_____ the Rev - e - la - tor. Book of _____ the sev - en seals. _____

Outro-Guitar Solo

Bkgd. Voc.: w/ Voc. ad lib.

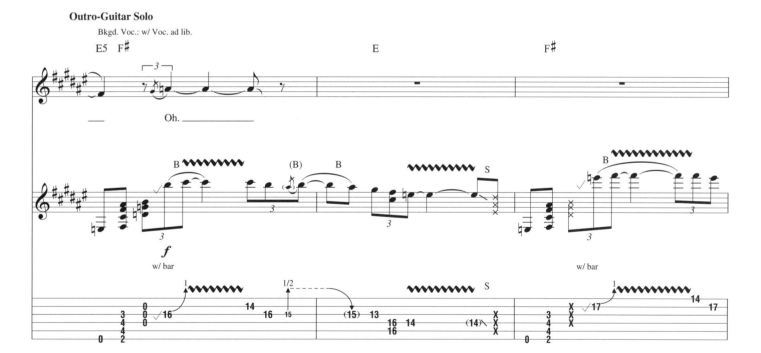

Oh.

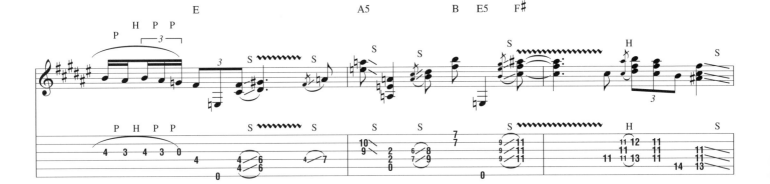

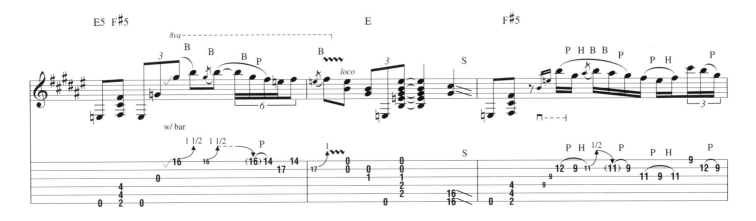

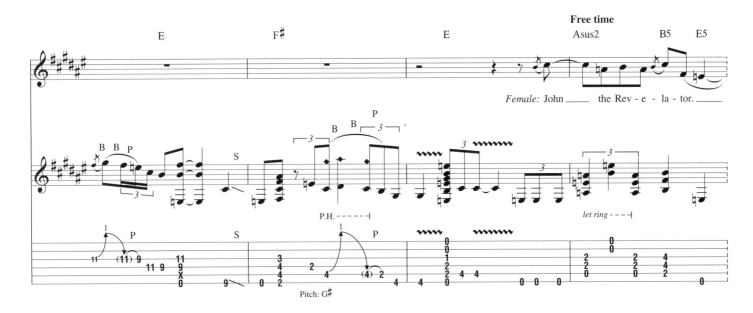

Segue to "Book of the Seven Seals"

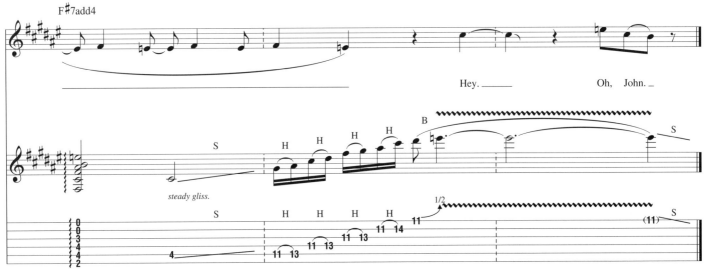

Book of the Seven Seals

By Steve Vai, Sean Ivory and Paul Caldwell

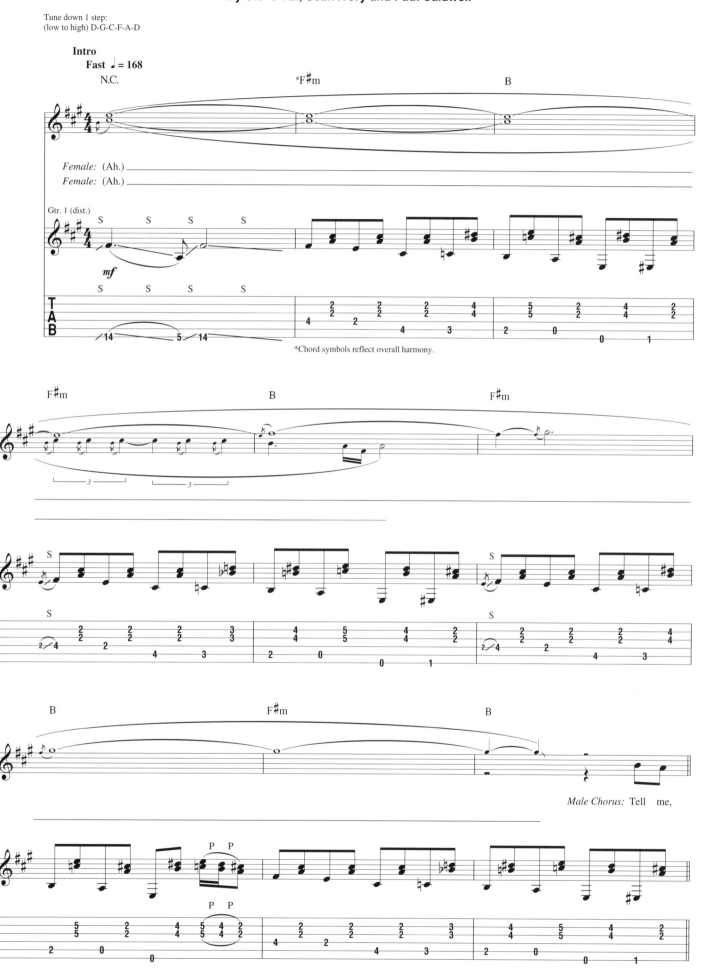

*Chord symbols reflect overall harmony.

what is he writ - ing?   Writ - ing in the book   of   sev - en   seals.__

'Bout   the Rev - e - la - tion. Writ - ing in the book   of   sev - en   seals.__

Guitar Solo

Pitch: G✕

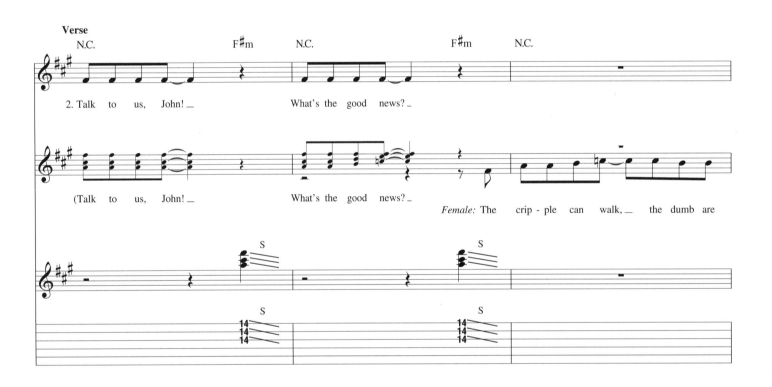

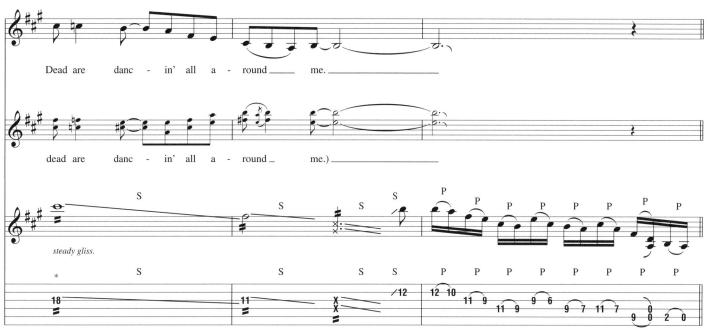

Dead are danc - in' all a - round _____ me. _____

dead are danc - in' all a - round _____ me.) _____

steady gliss.

*Pick sixteenth-notes while sliding.

Interlude

Bkgd. Voc.: w/ Voc. ad lib.

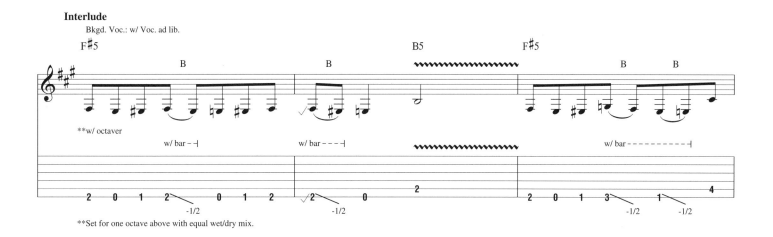

**w/ octaver

**Set for one octave above with equal wet/dry mix.

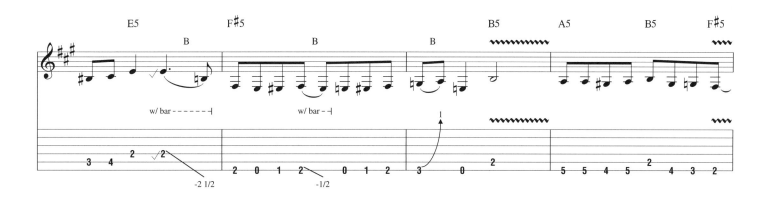

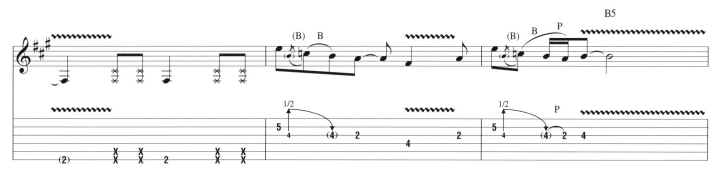

Bridge

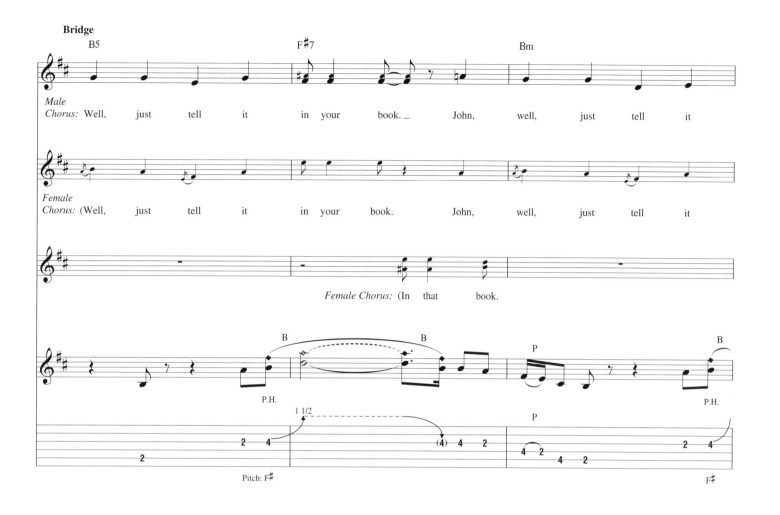

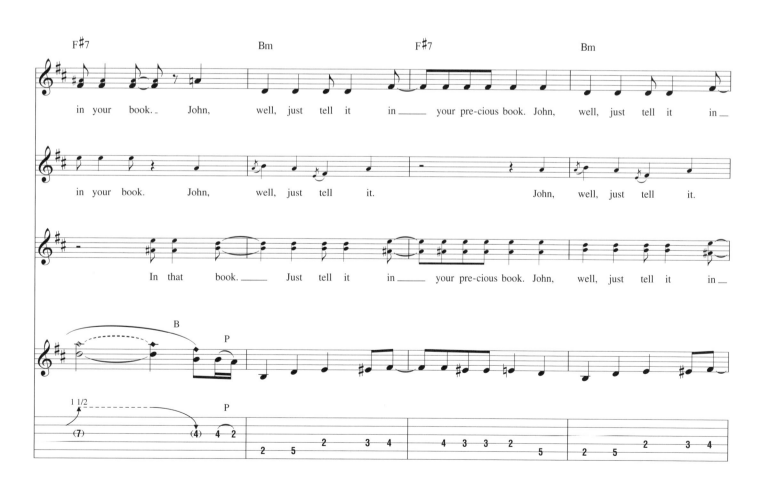

Outro

Bm

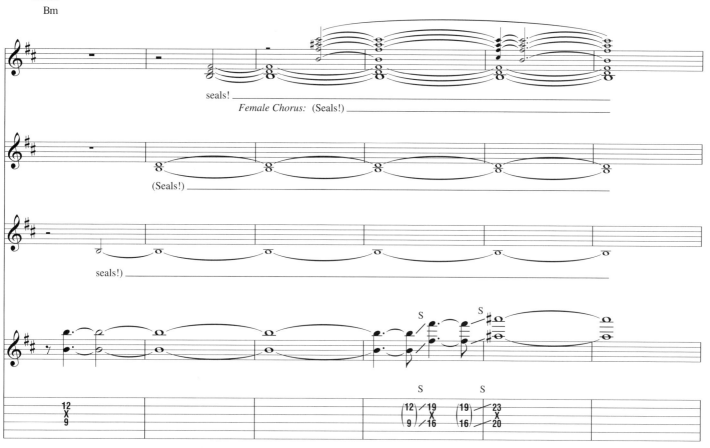

seals!

Female Chorus: (Seals!)

(Seals!)

seals!)

Free time

N.C.

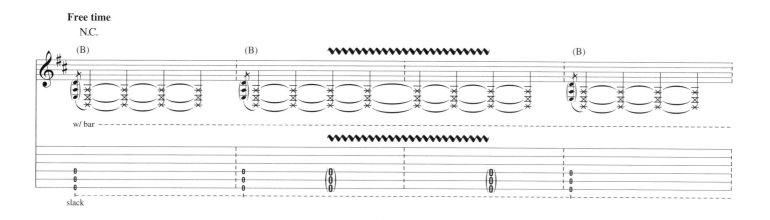

w/ bar

slack

Who _____ is writ - ing?

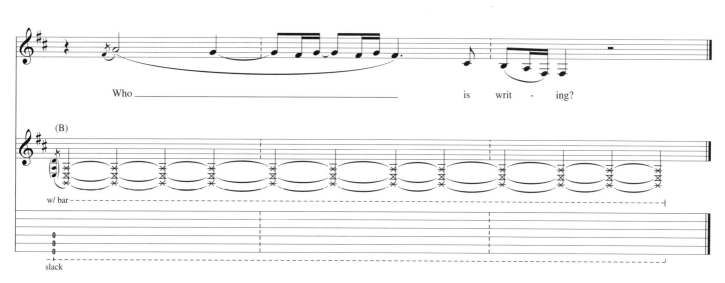

w/ bar

slack

75

Creamsicle Sunset

By Steve Vai

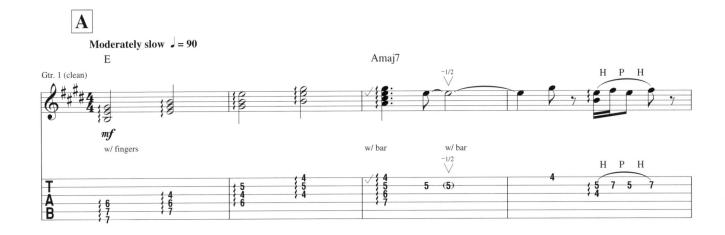

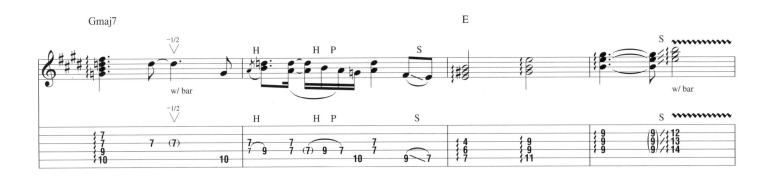

*Chord symbols reflect overall harmony.

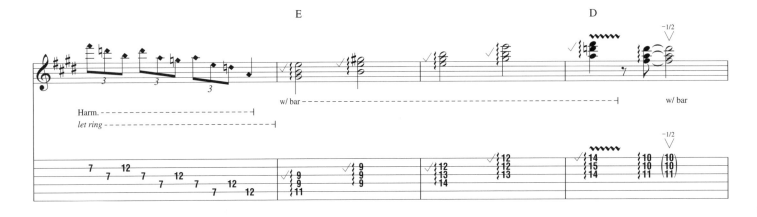

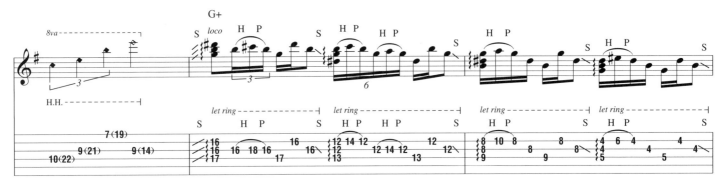

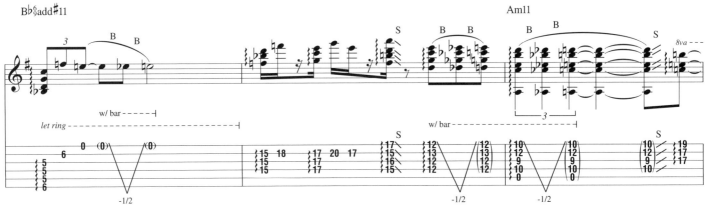

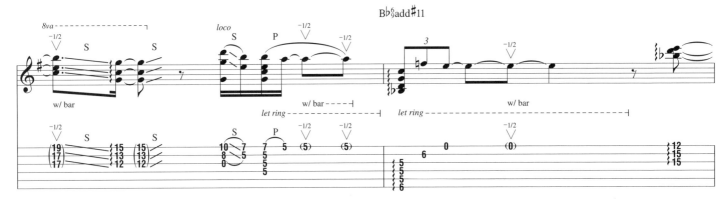

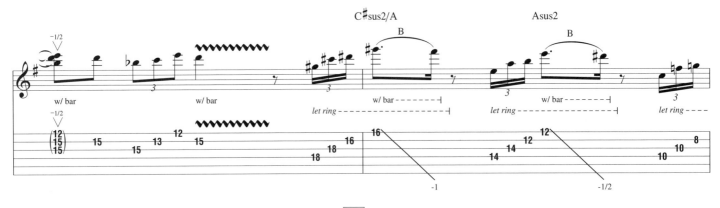

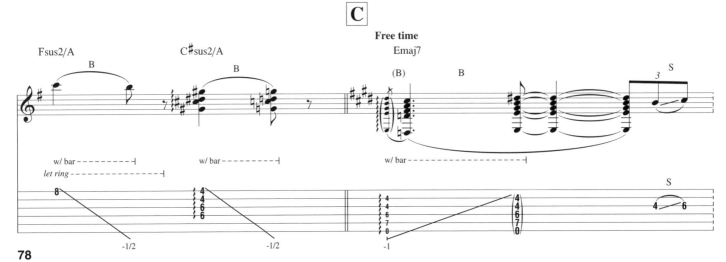

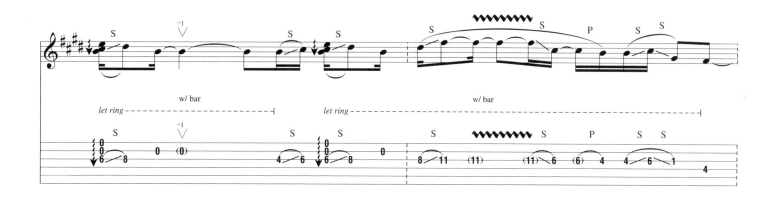
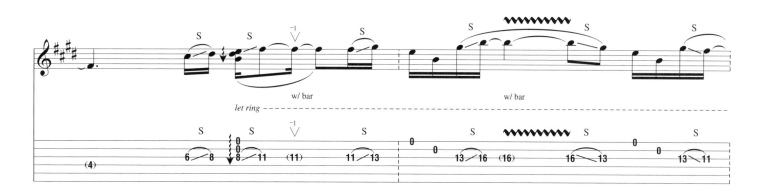
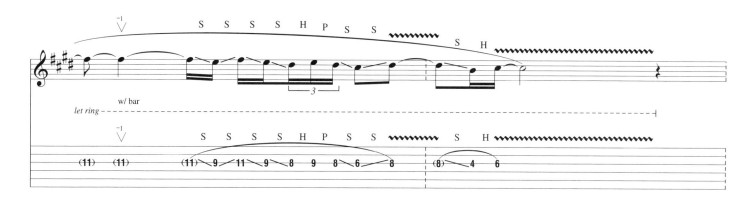
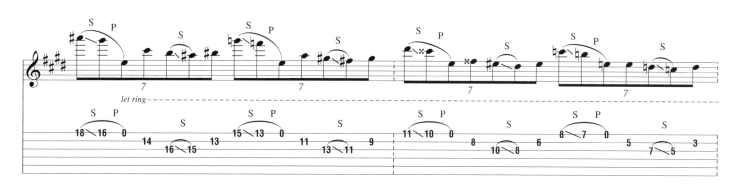

Gravity Storm

By Steve Vai

Tune down 1 step:
(low to high) D-G-C-F-A-D

81

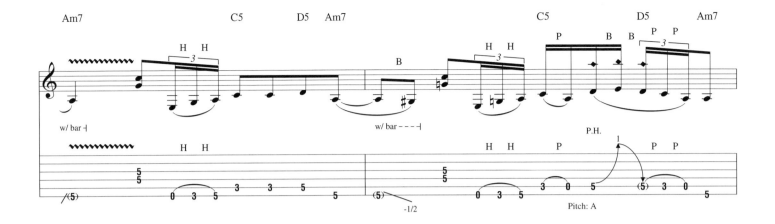

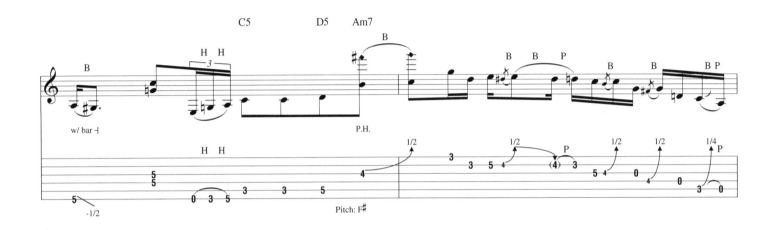

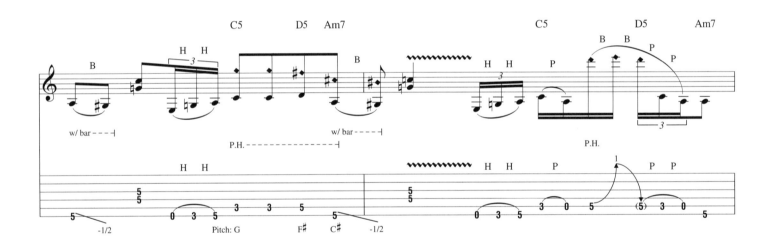

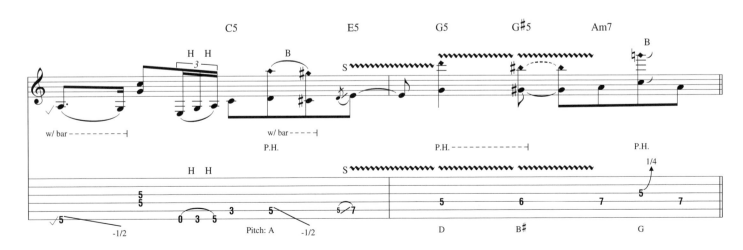

Em7

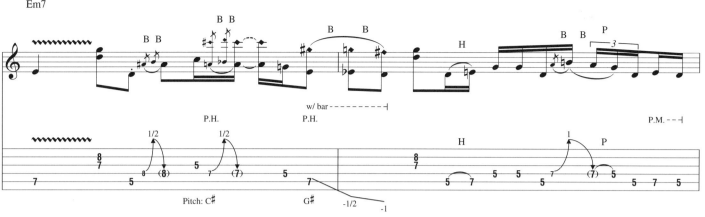

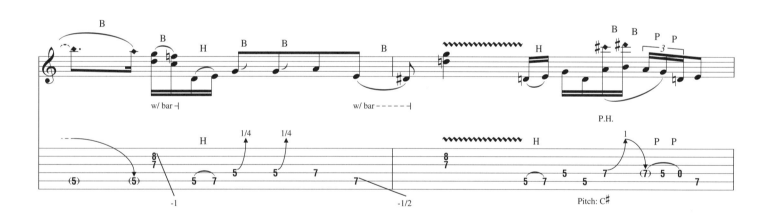

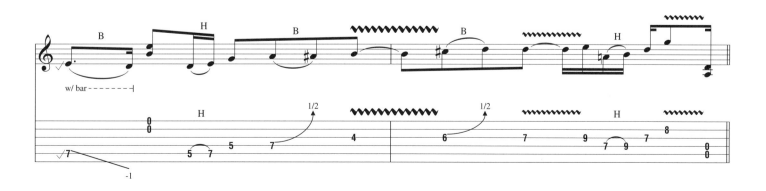

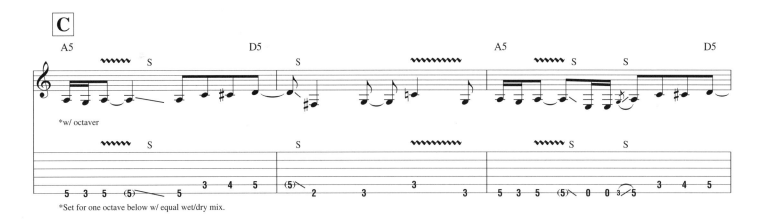

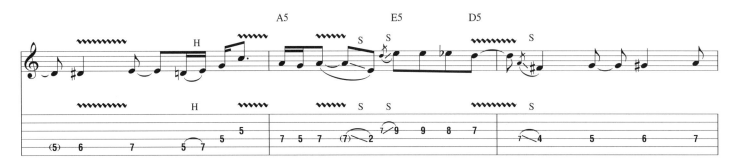

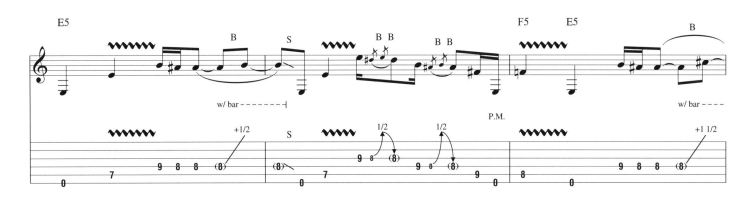

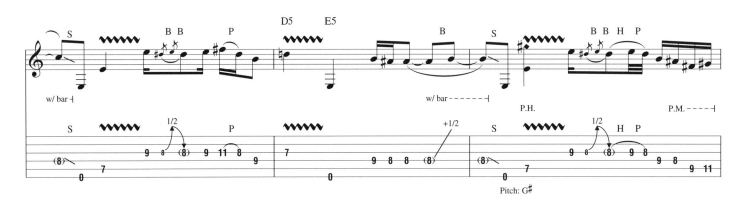

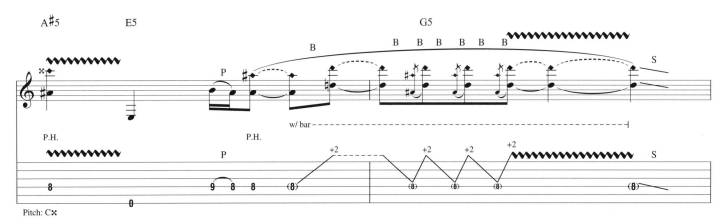

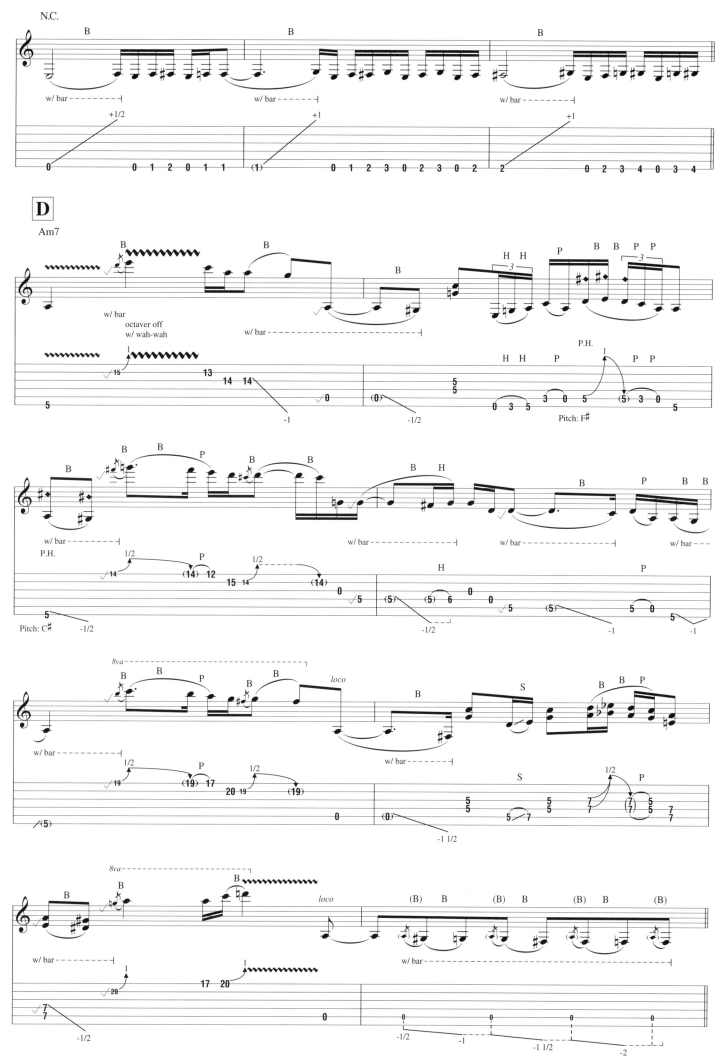

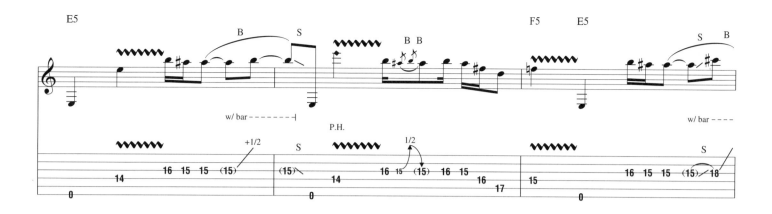

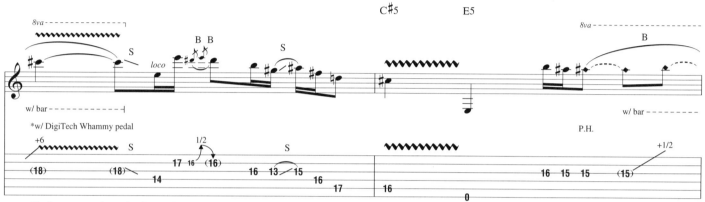

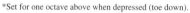

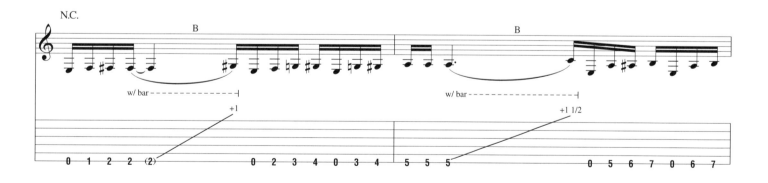

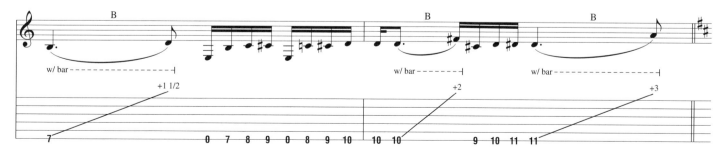

G

Bm7

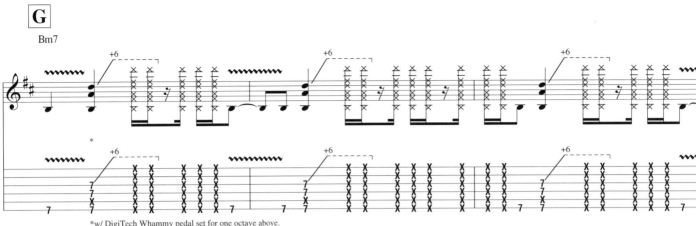

*w/ DigiTech Whammy pedal set for one octave above.
Guitar signal split (Whammy and dry) 50/50.

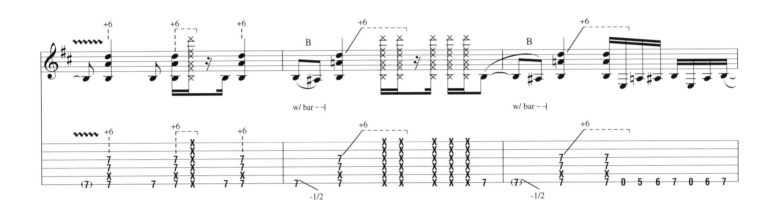

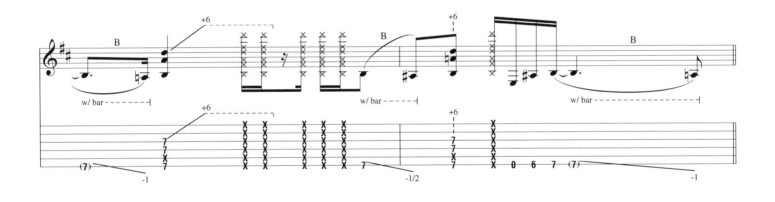

H

B5

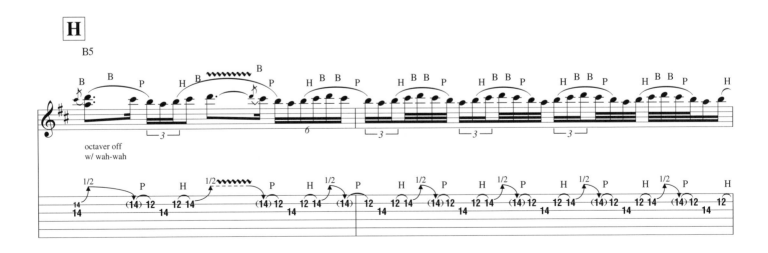

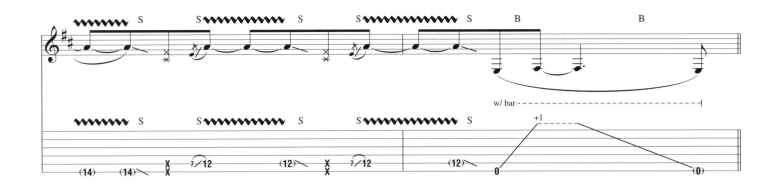

I

B5

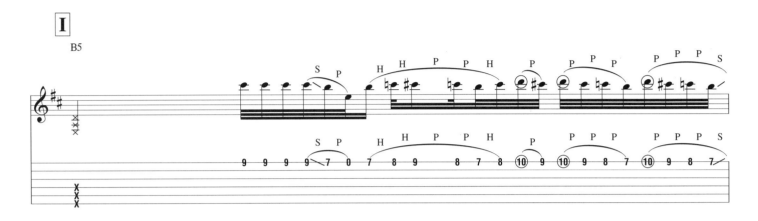

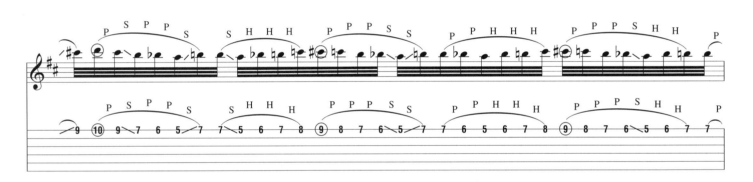

*Slide tap finger.

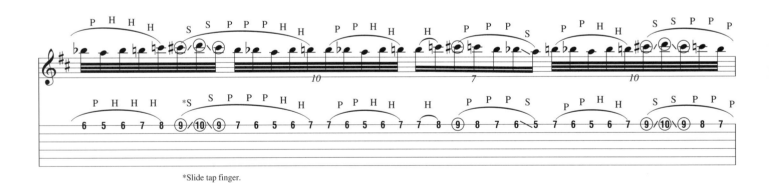

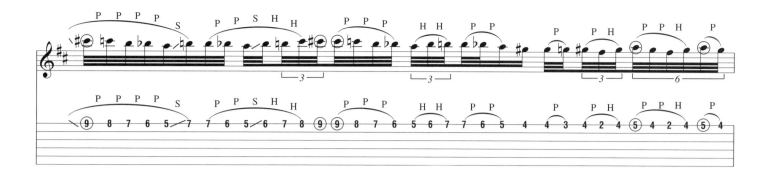

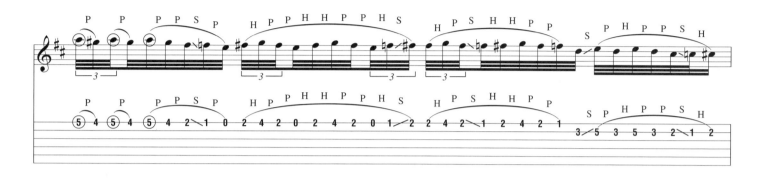

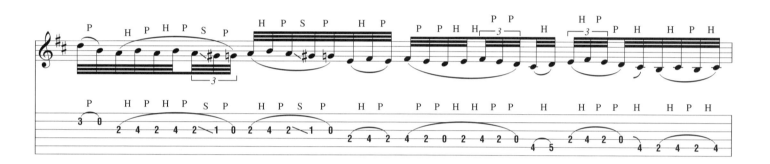

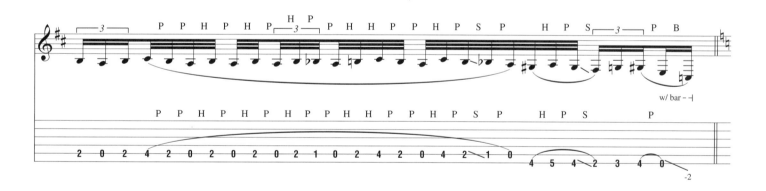

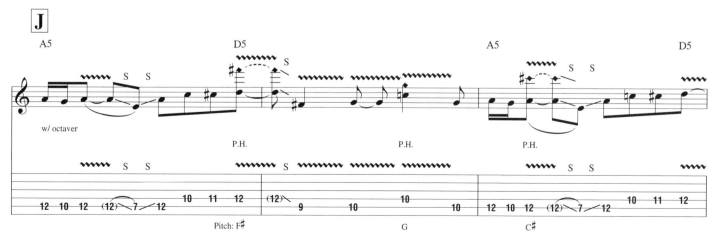

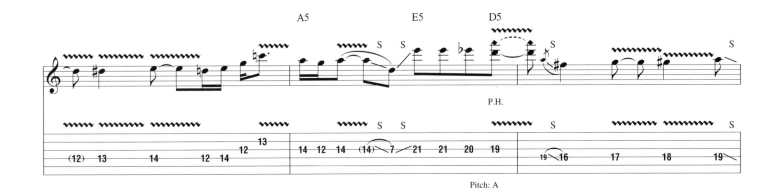

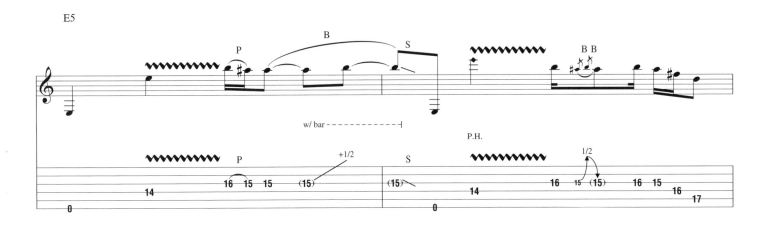

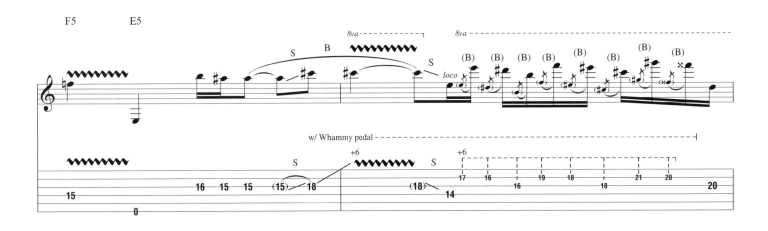

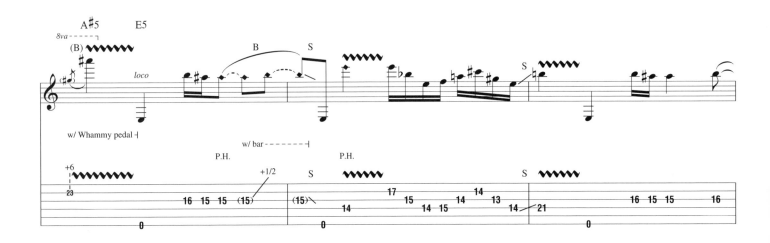

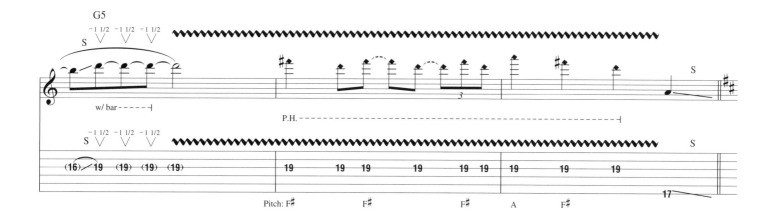

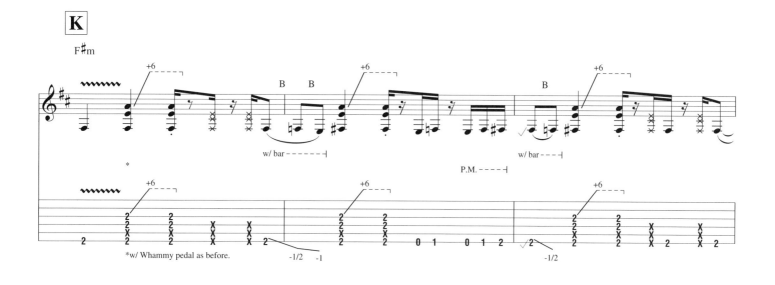

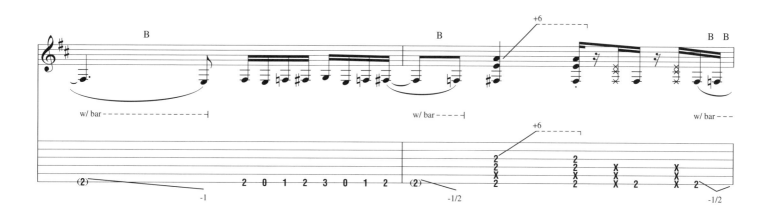

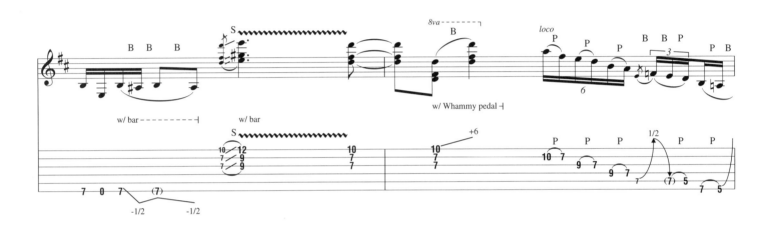

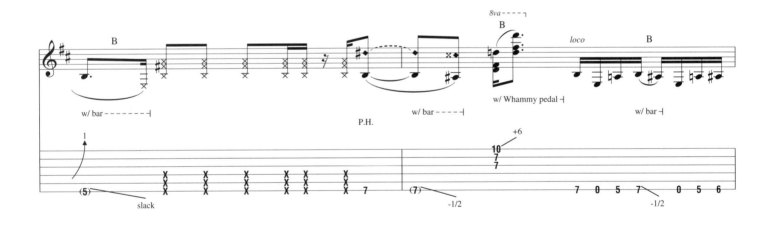

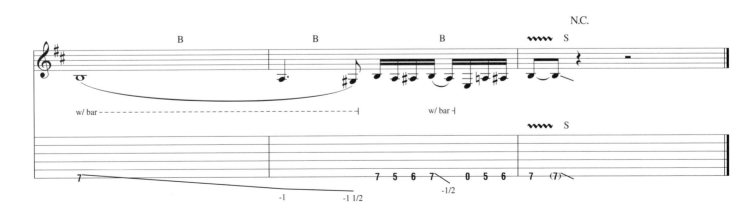

Mullach a' tSí

Traditional Irish Lullaby
Arrangement by Steve Vai

Gtr. 1: Drop A tuning:
(low to high) A-E-A-D-G-B-E

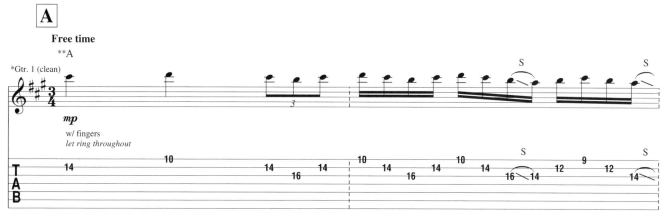

*7-str. elec.   **Chord symbols reflect basic harmony.

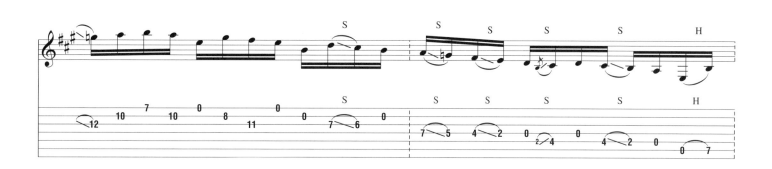

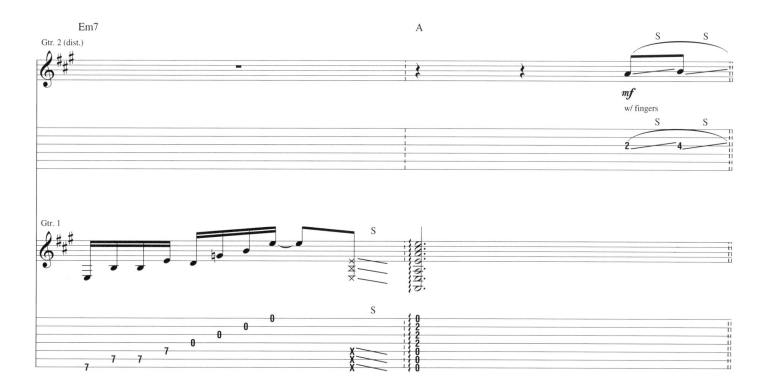

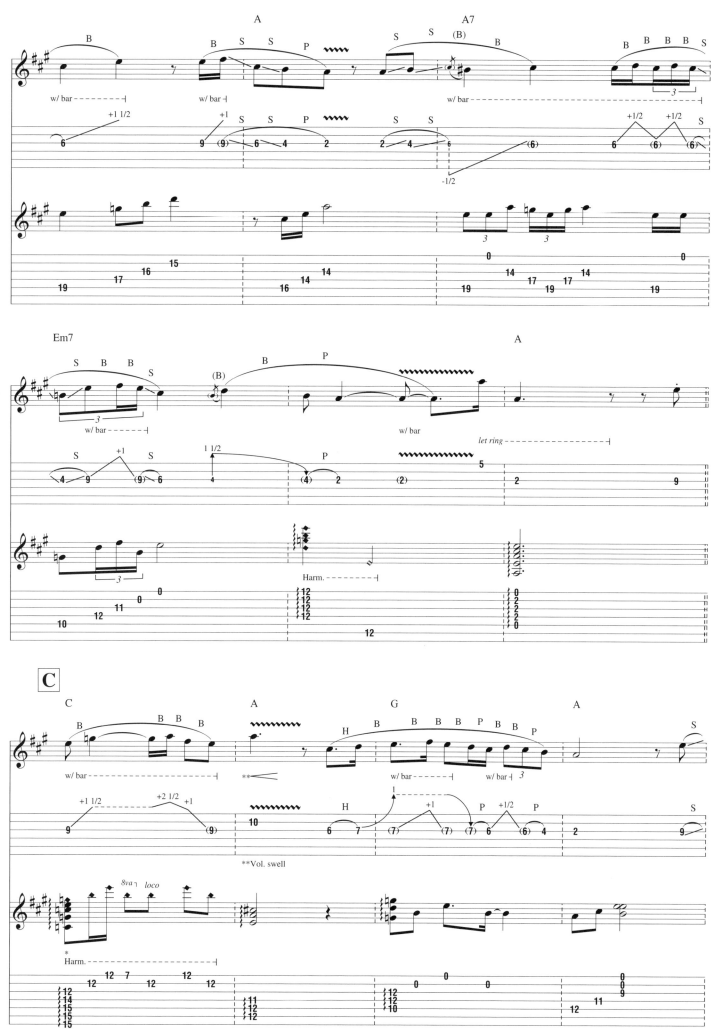

*Fret chord notes normally with fret-hand fingers. Reach fret-hand thumb under
   and in front of neck to lightly touch strings 1, 2 & 3 at 12th fret for natural harmonics.

The Moon and I

By Steve Vai

Intro
Moderately fast ♩ = 141

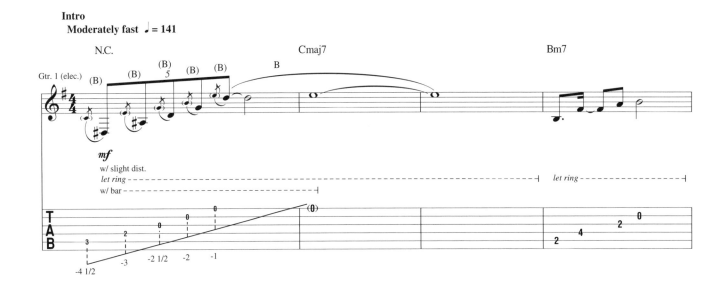

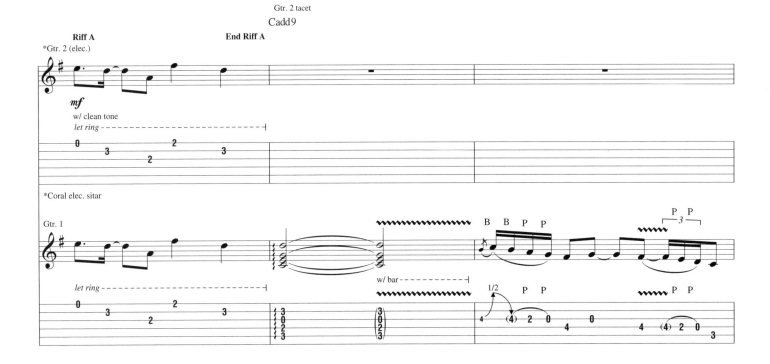

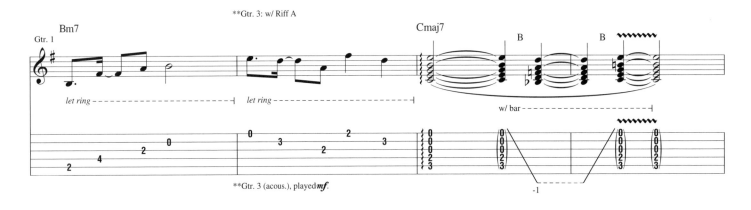

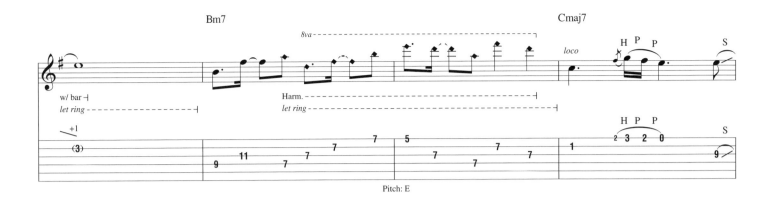

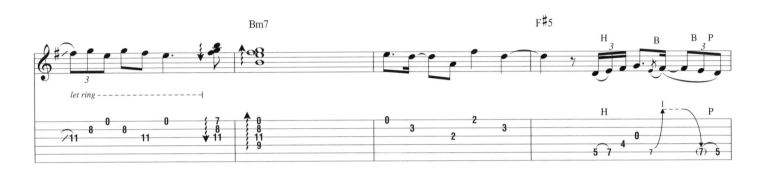

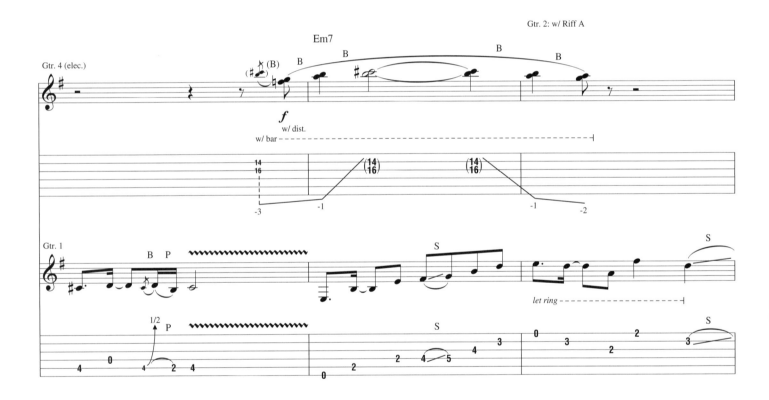

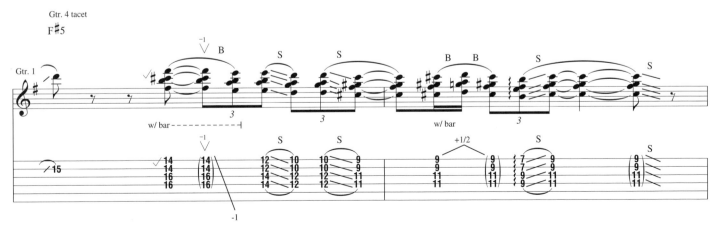

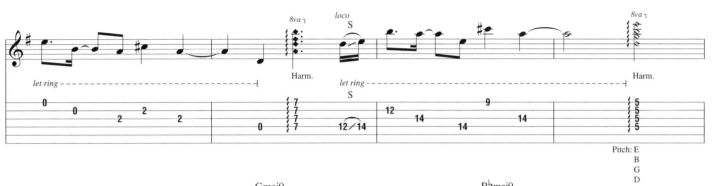

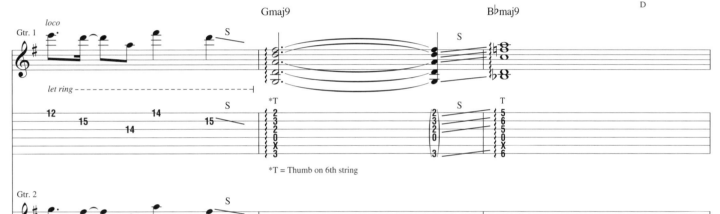

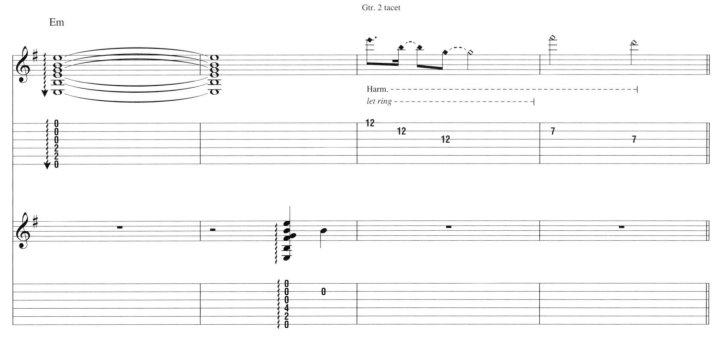

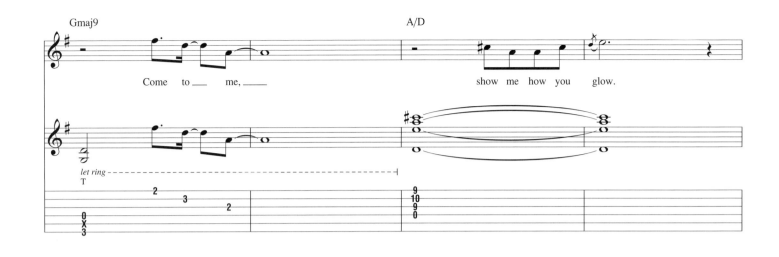

Come to me, ____ show me how you glow.

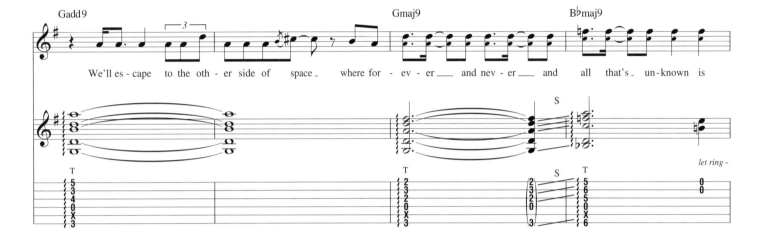

We'll es-cape to the oth-er side of space ___ where for- ev- er ___ and nev- er ___ and all that's __ un-known is

Gtr. 3: w/ Riff B

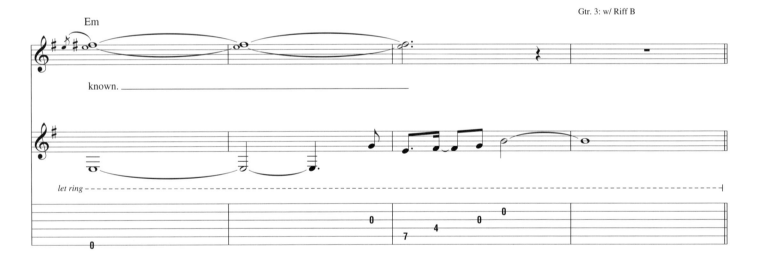

known. _____

Guitar Solo

Gtrs. 1 & 2 tacet

C5   B5

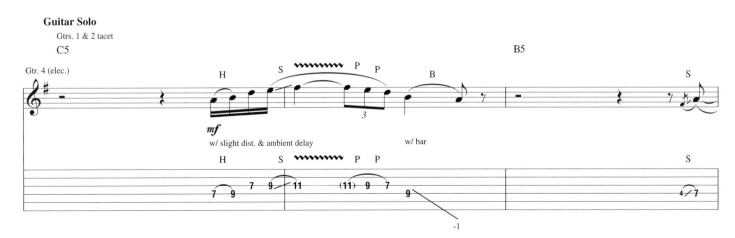

Gtr. 4 (elec.)

mf

w/ slight dist. & ambient delay   w/ bar

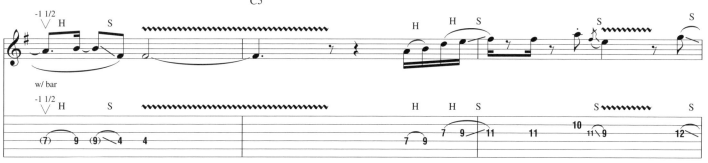

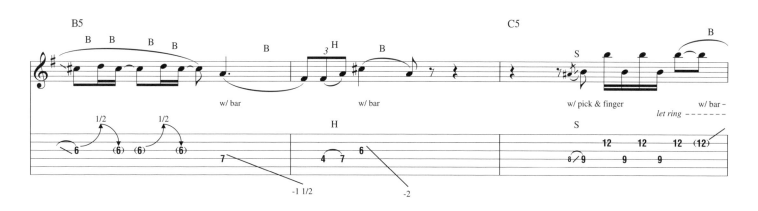

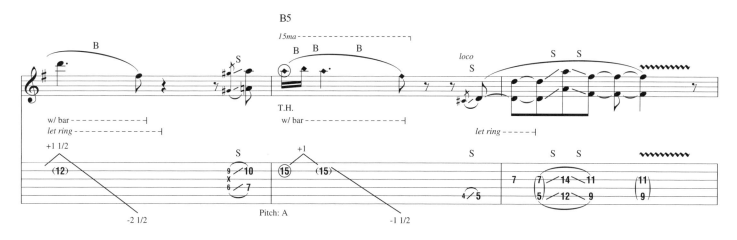

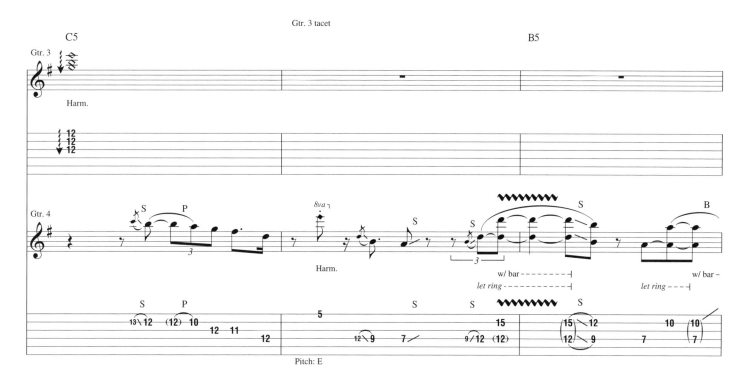

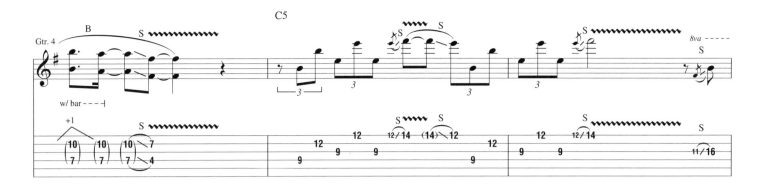
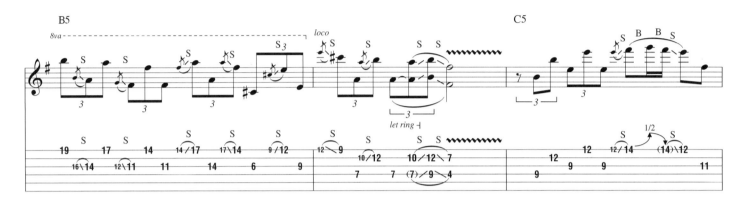
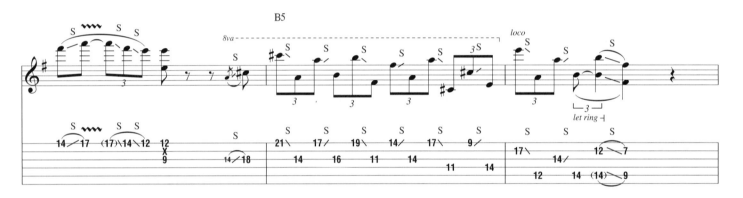
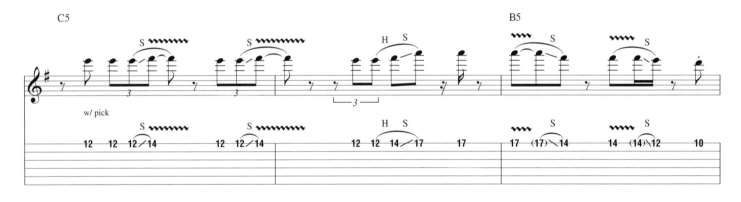
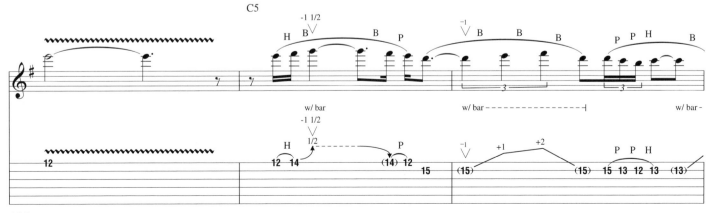

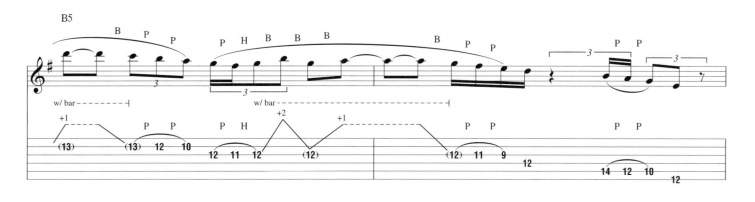

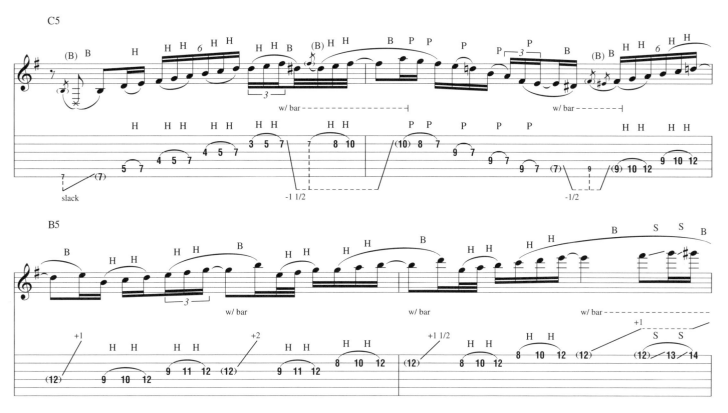

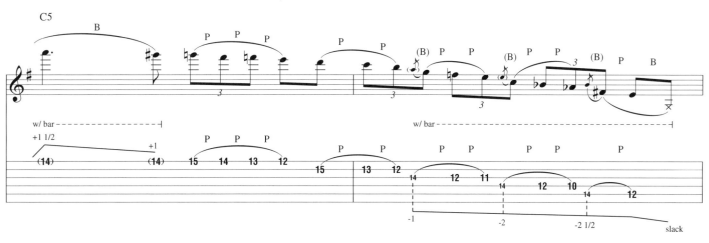

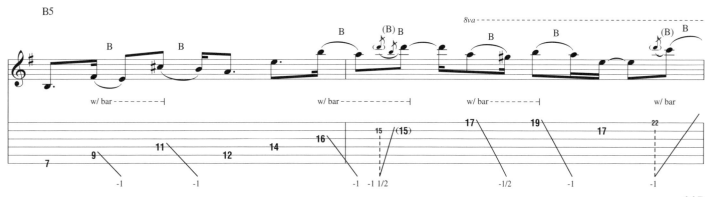

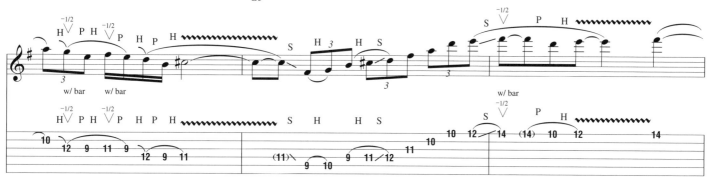

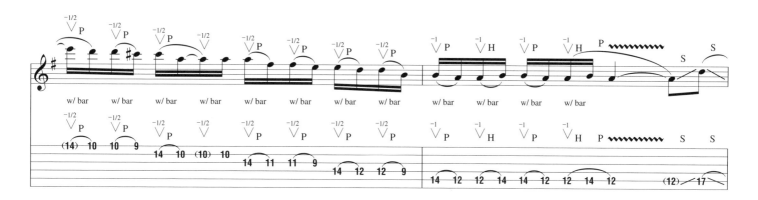

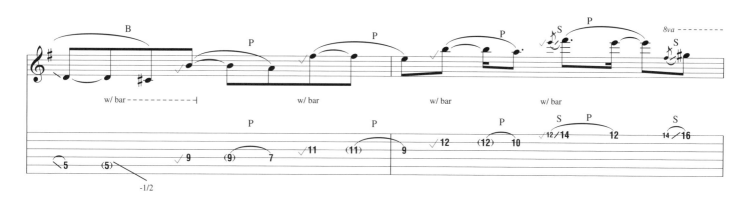

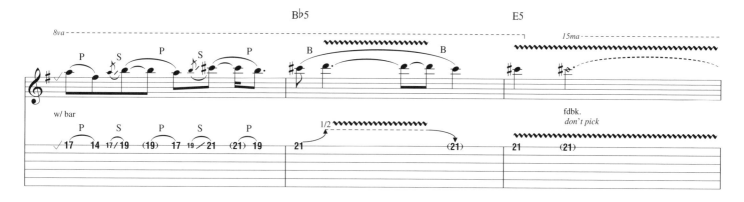

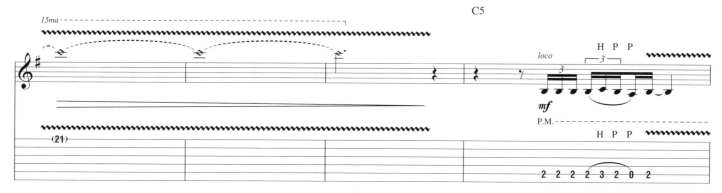

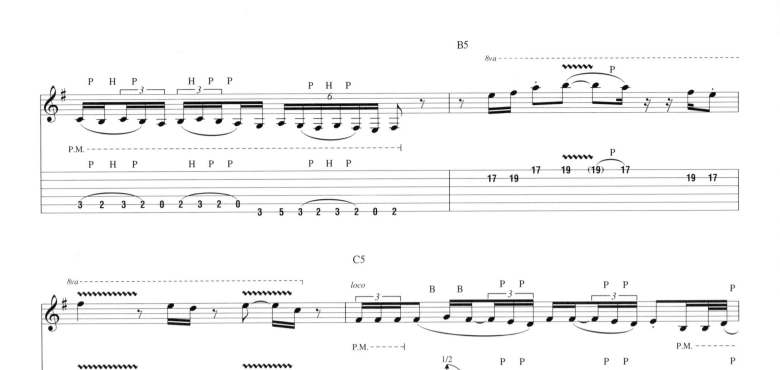

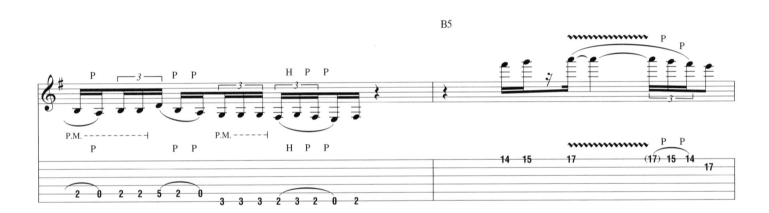

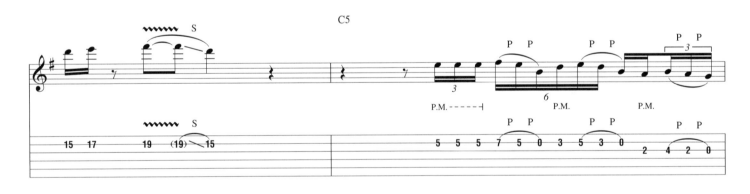

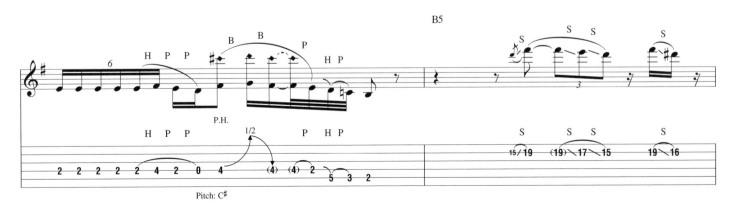

Pitch: C#

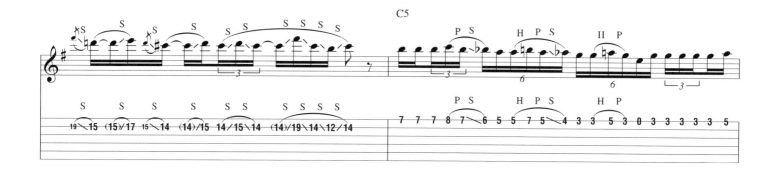

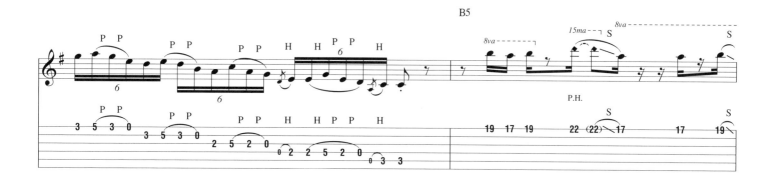

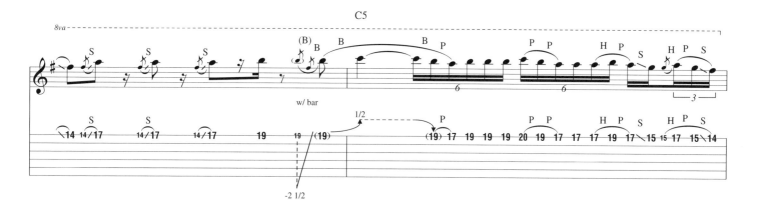

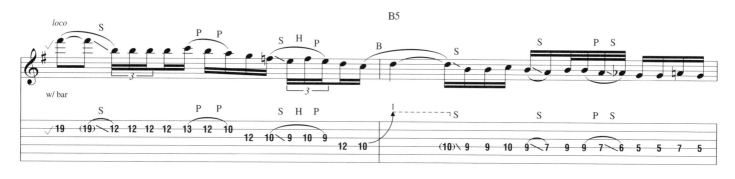

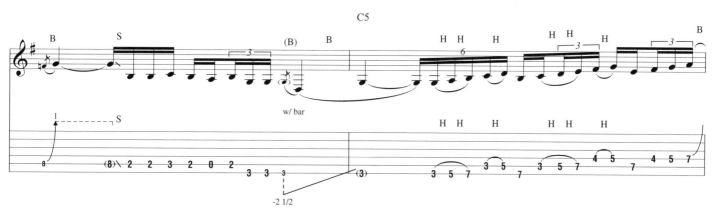

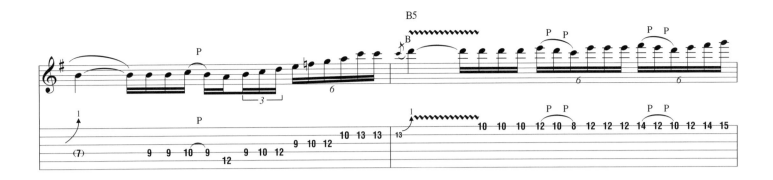

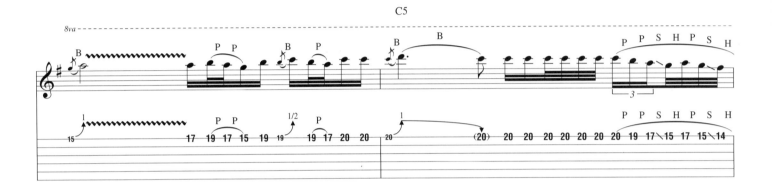

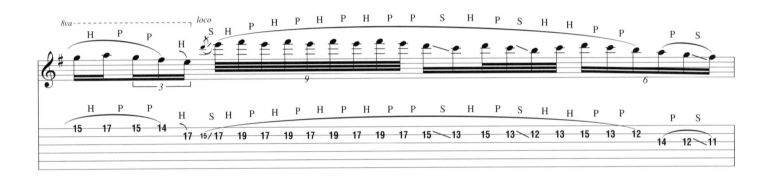

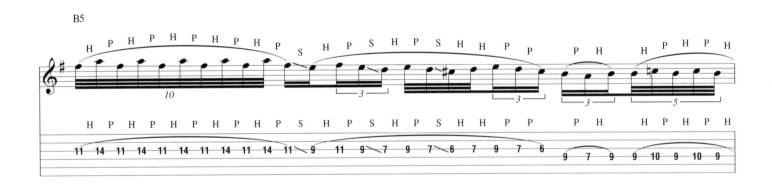

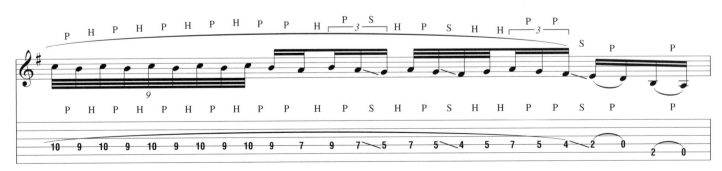

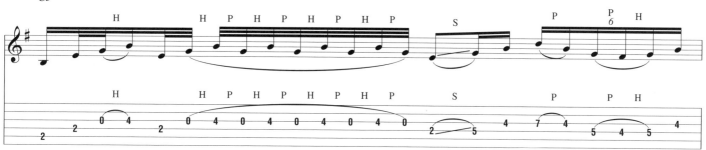

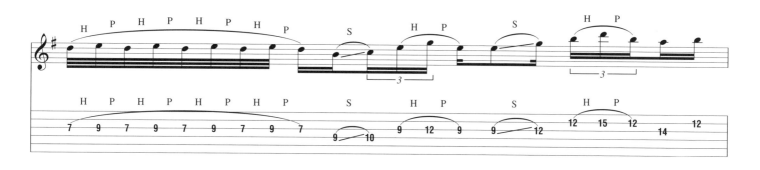

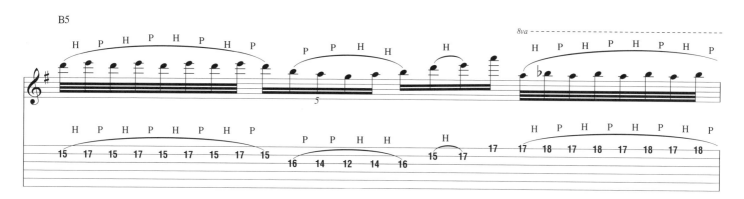

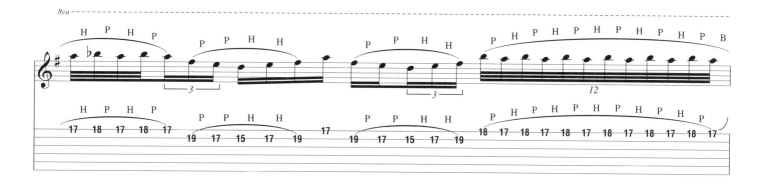

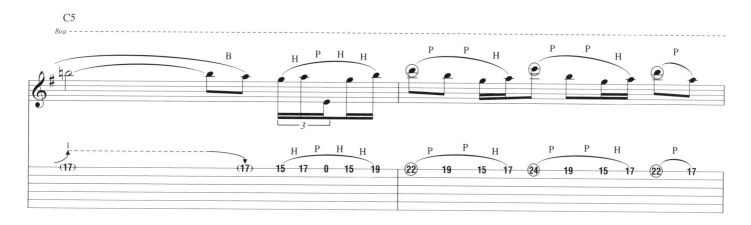

121

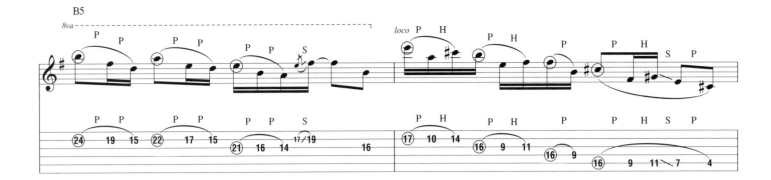

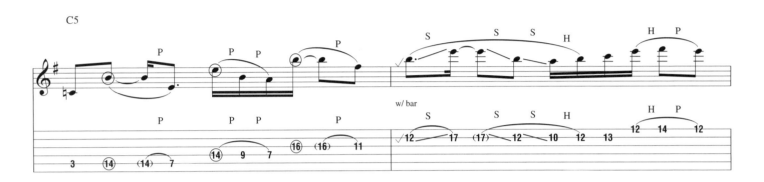

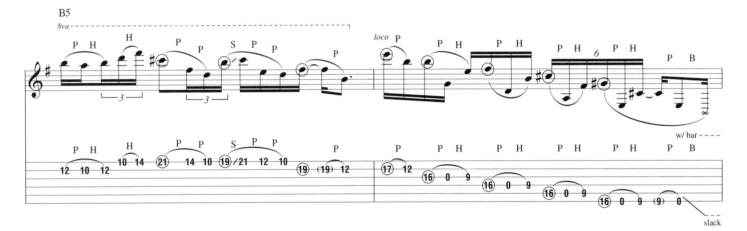

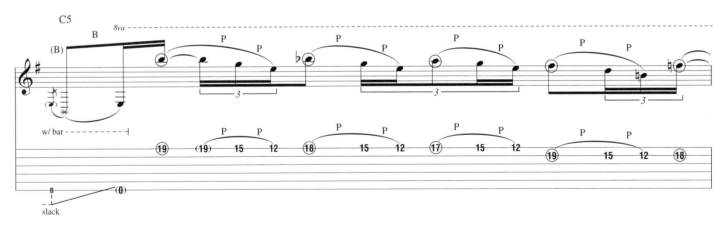

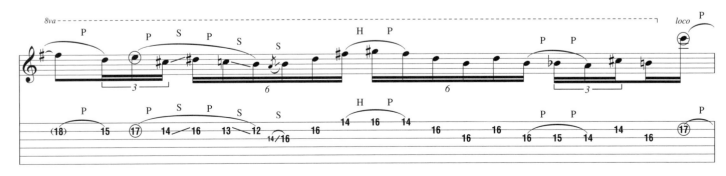

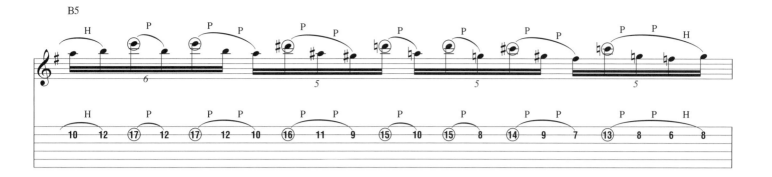

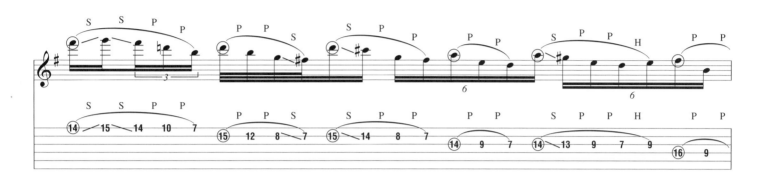

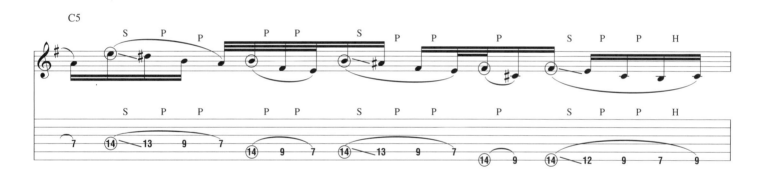

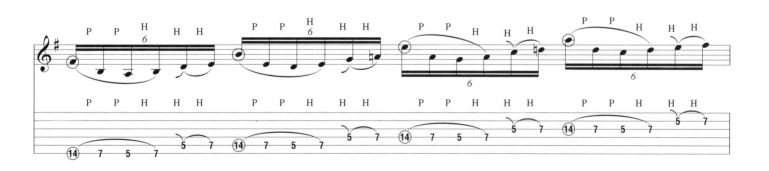

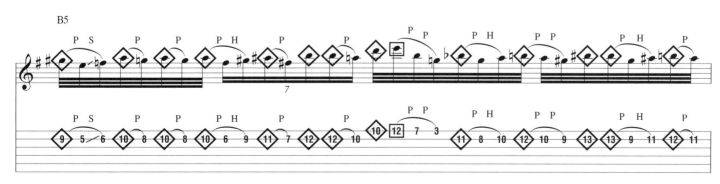

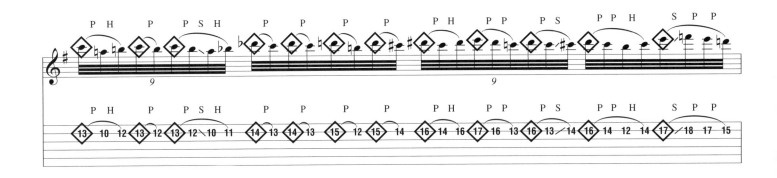

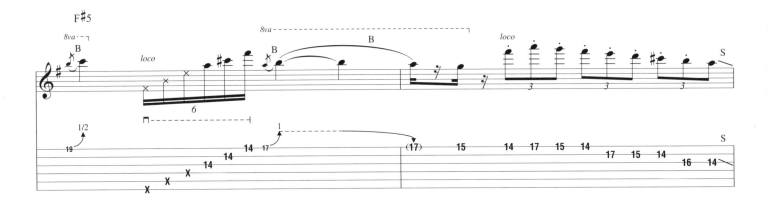

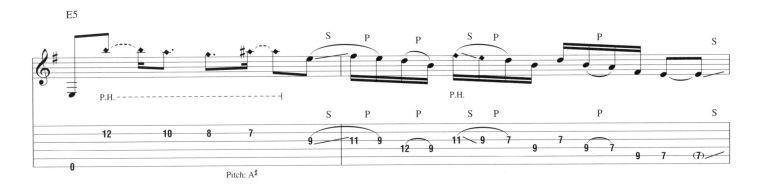

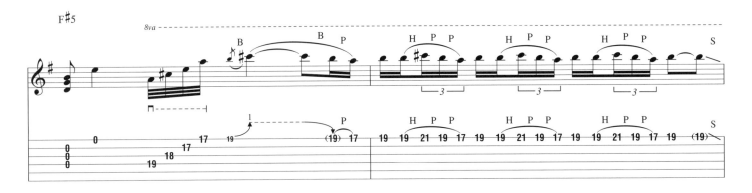

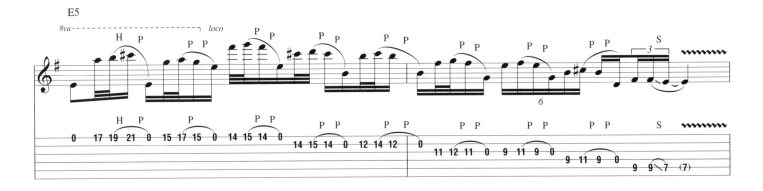

G5

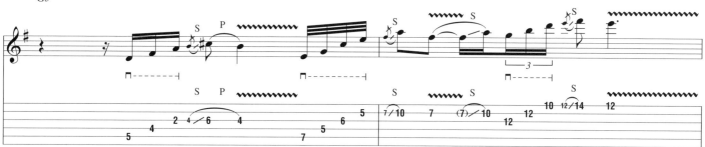

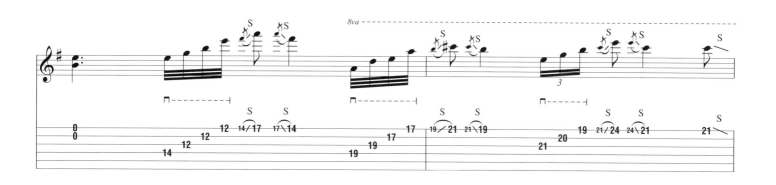

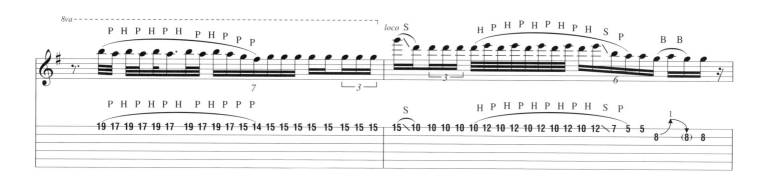

Bb5

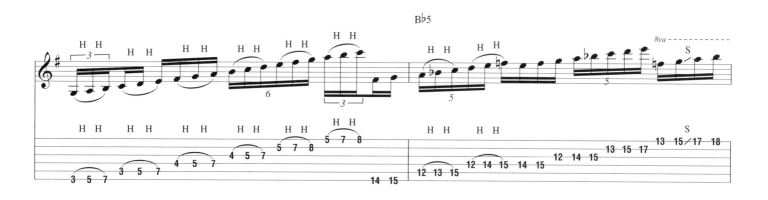

E5

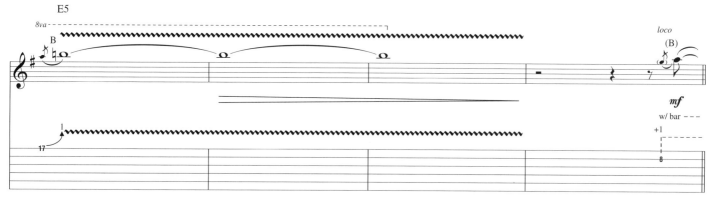

Outro

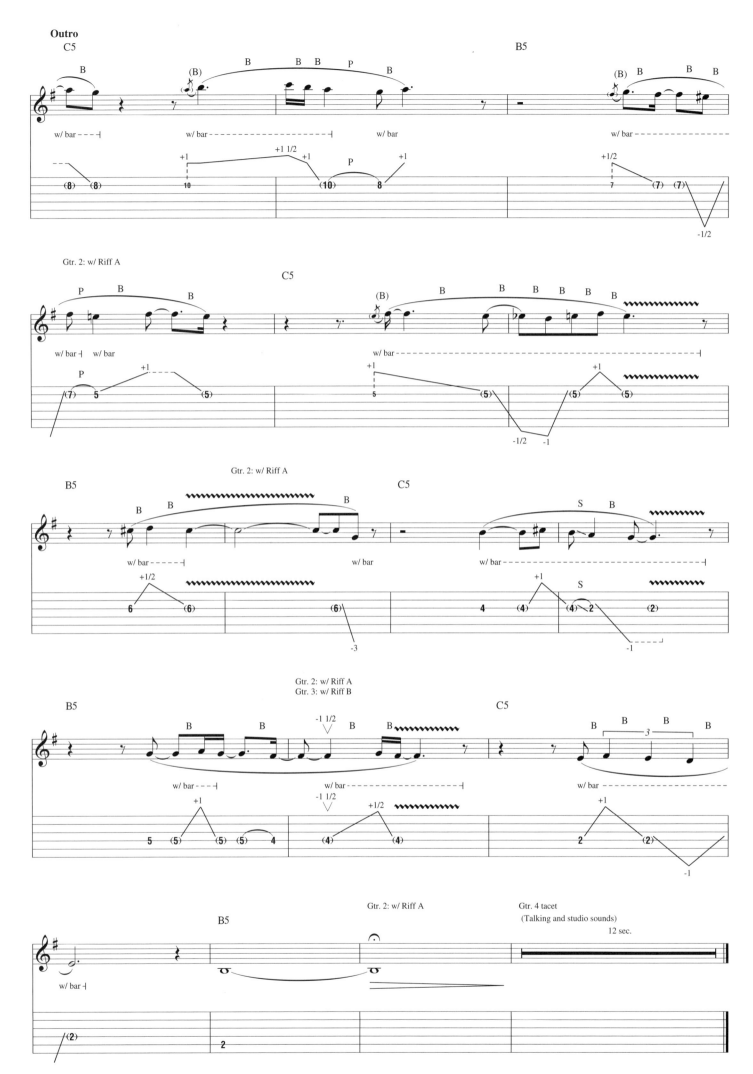

Weeping China Doll

By Steve Vai

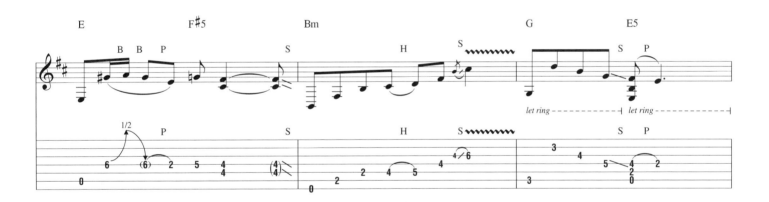

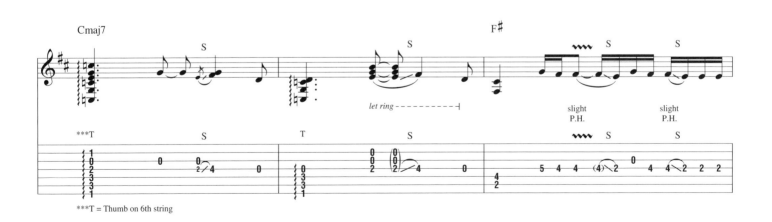

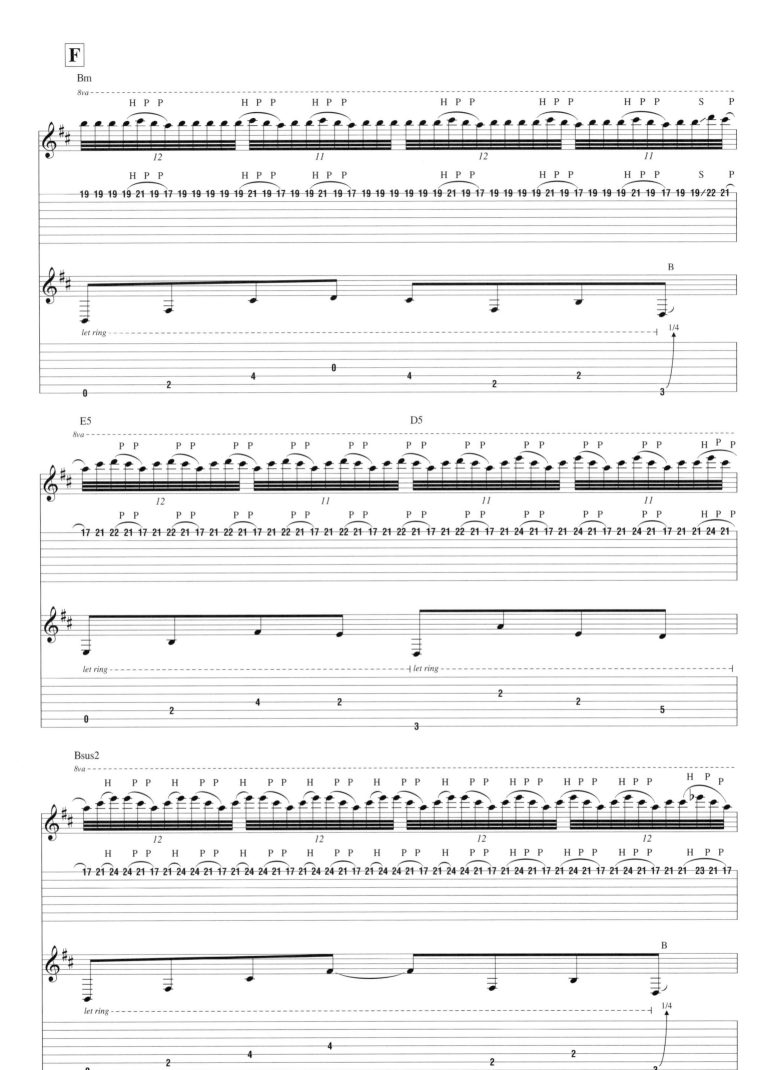

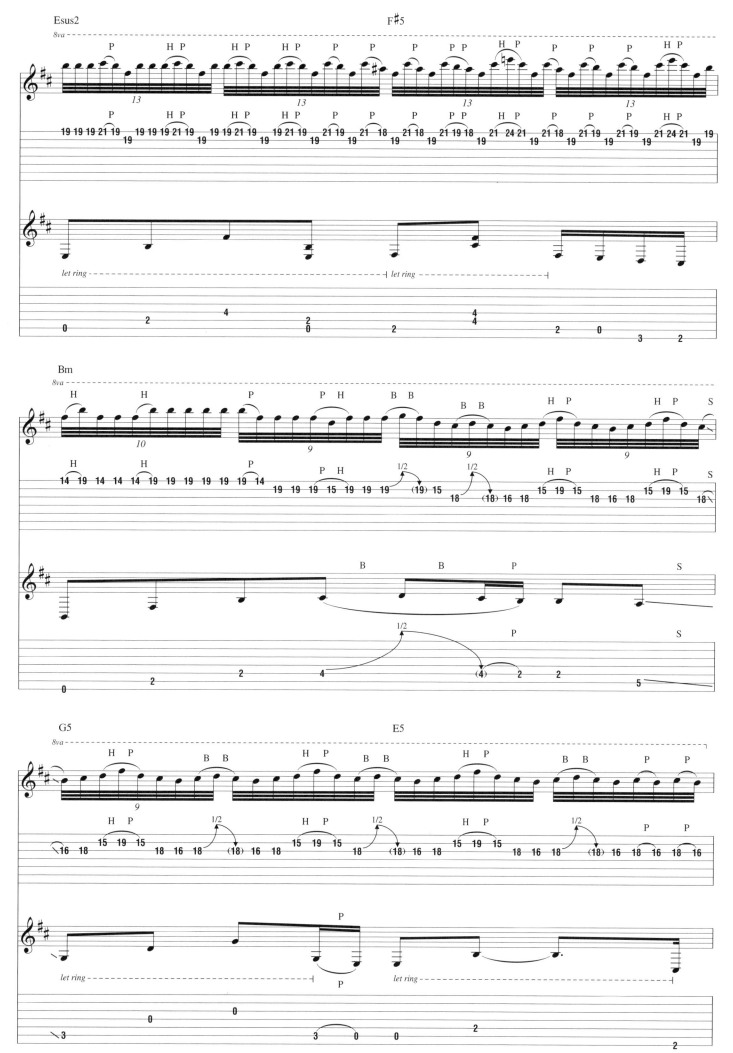

136

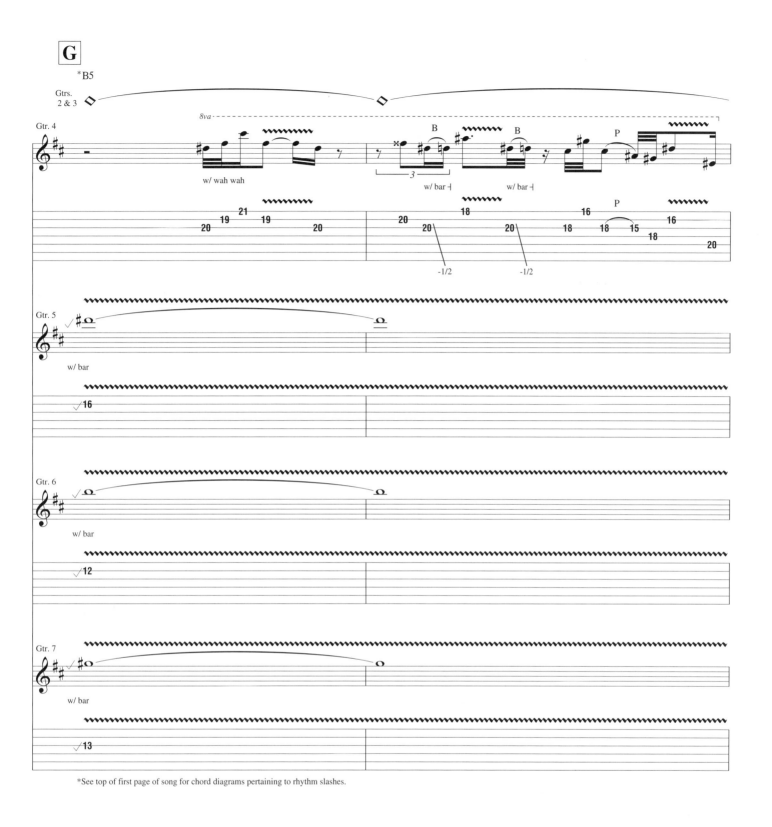

*See top of first page of song for chord diagrams pertaining to rhythm slashes.

Gtrs. 5, 6 & 7 tacet

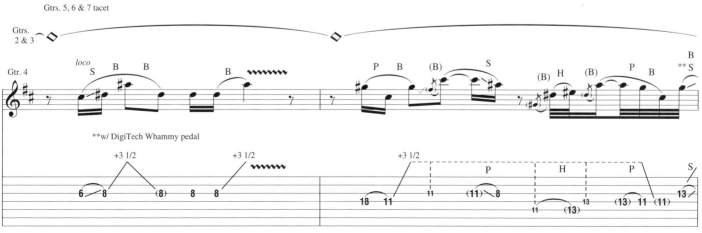

**w/ DigiTech Whammy pedal

**Set for perfect fifth above when depressed (toe down).

**Depress Whammy pedal and execute slide simultaneously.

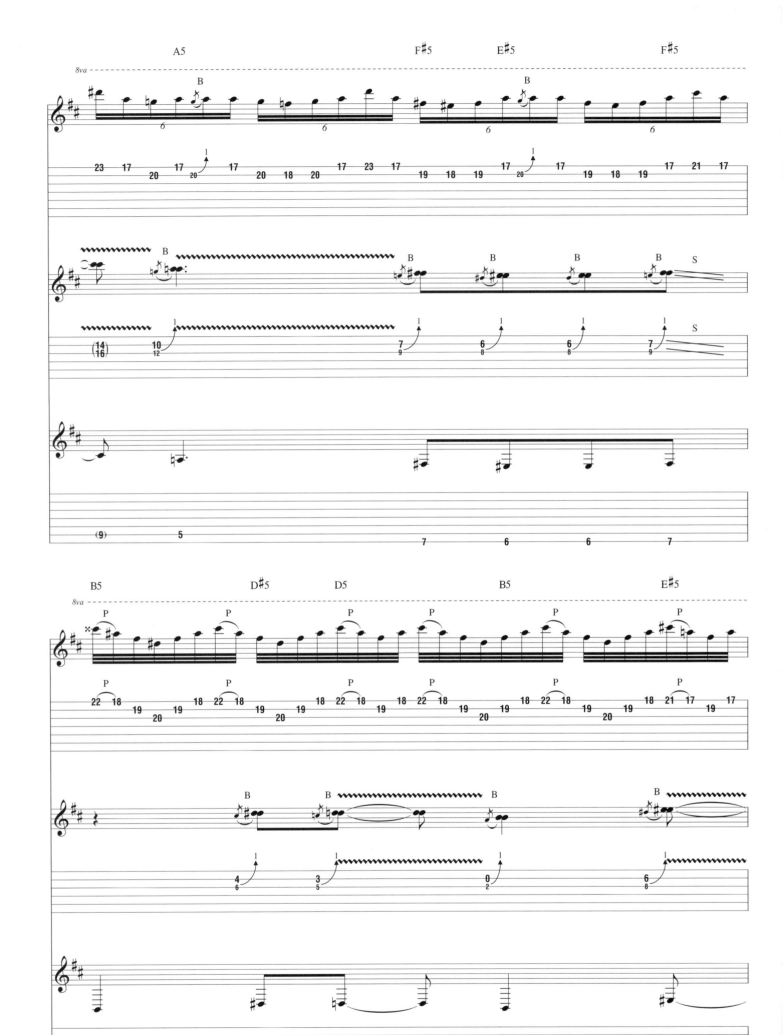

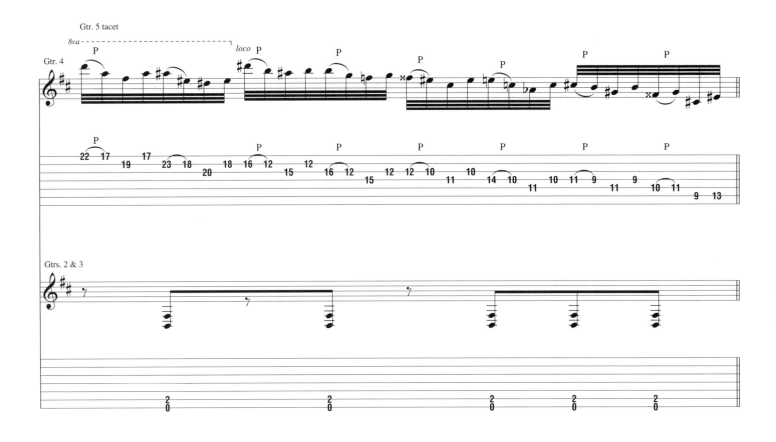

I

C#

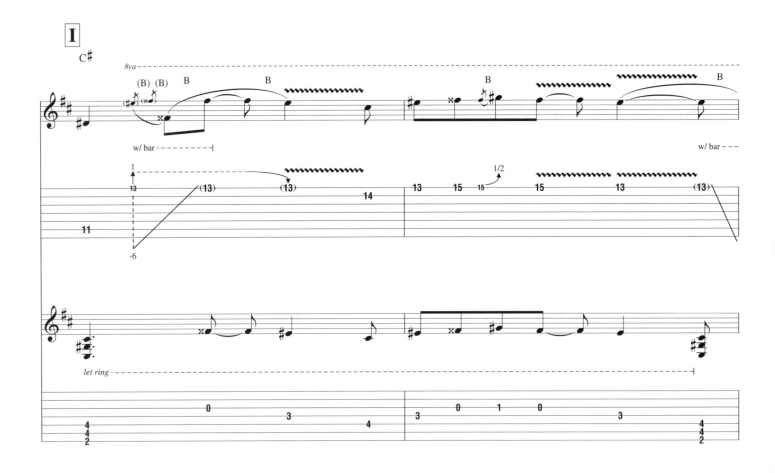

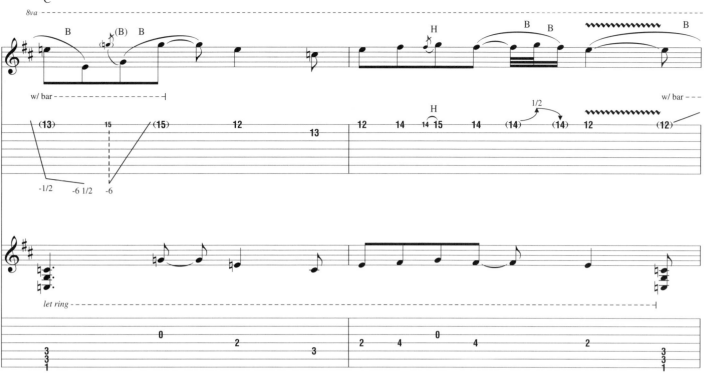

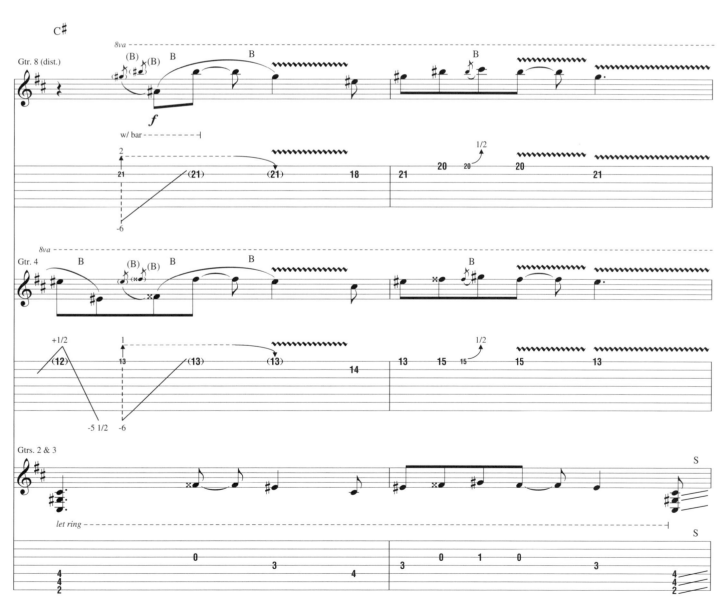

146

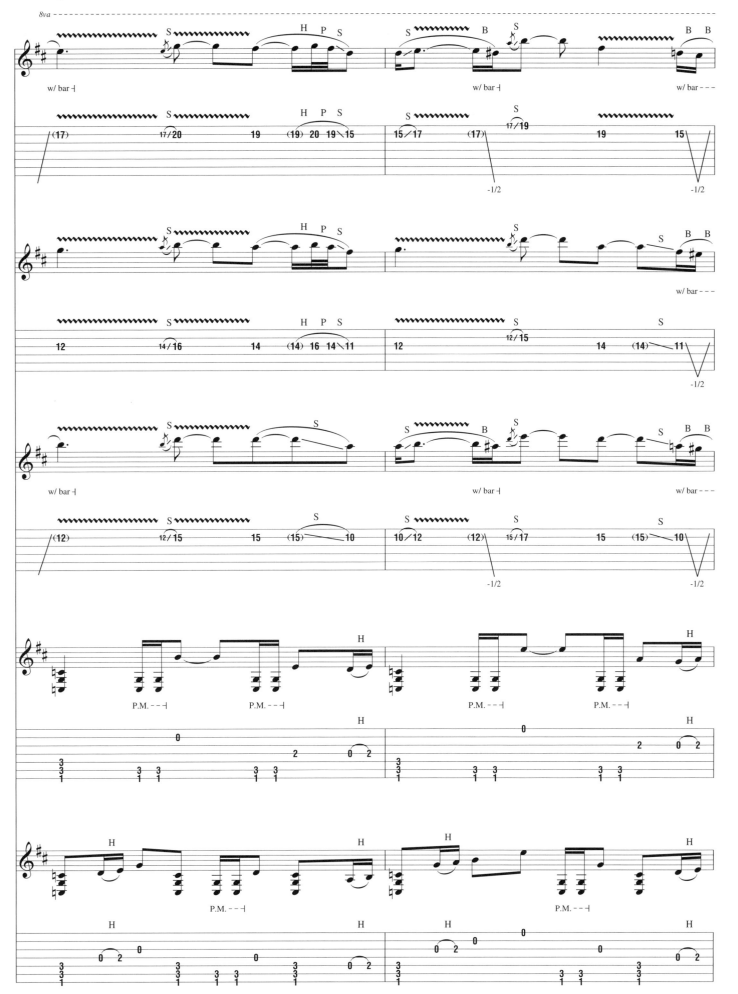

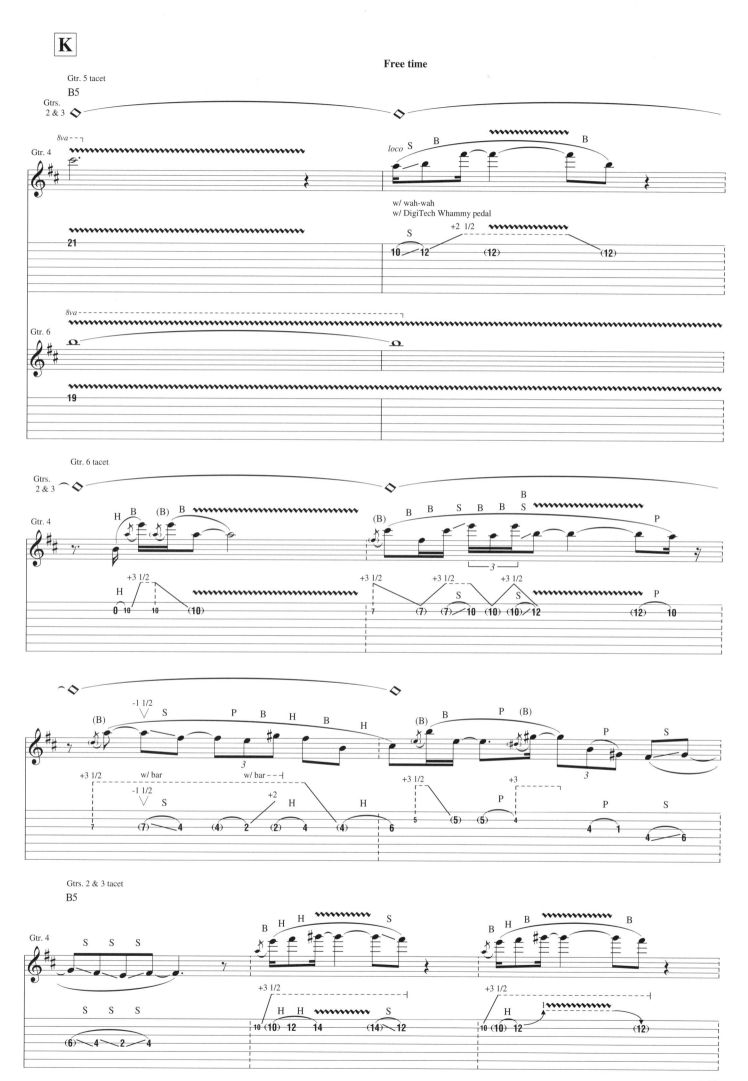

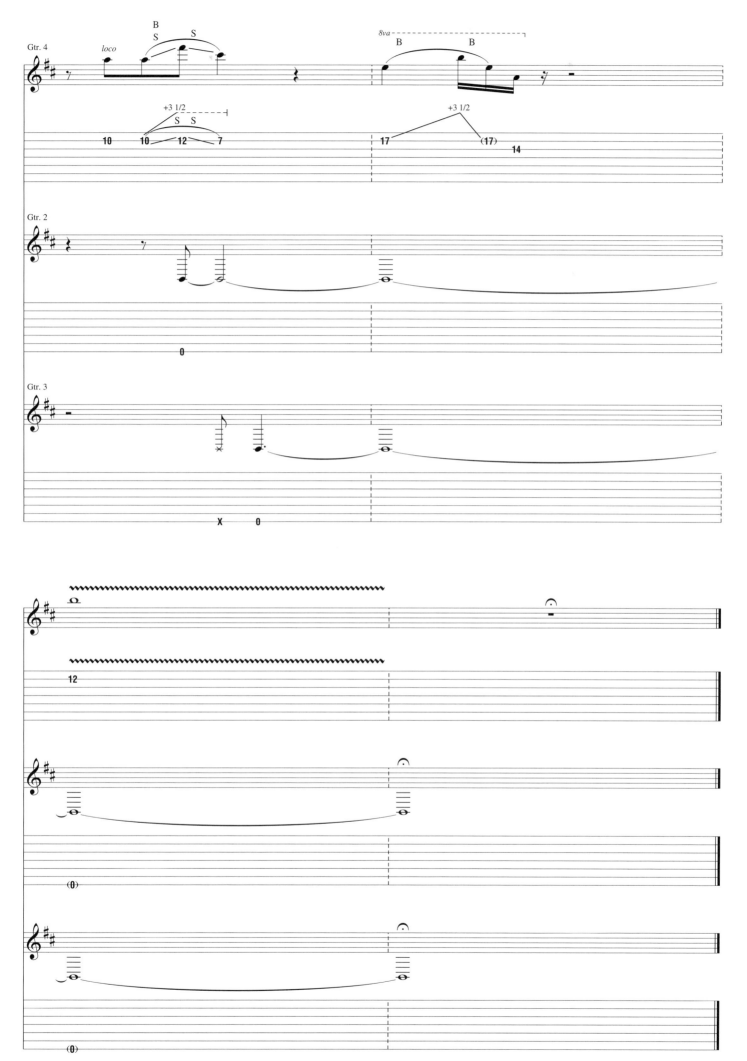

Racing the World

By Steve Vai

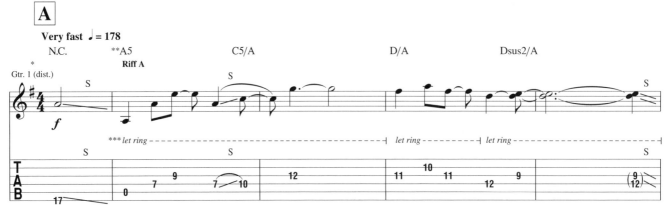

*Key signature denotes A Dorian (next 21 meas.).
**Chord symbols reflect implied harmony.
***Let open 5th string ring for 6 meas.

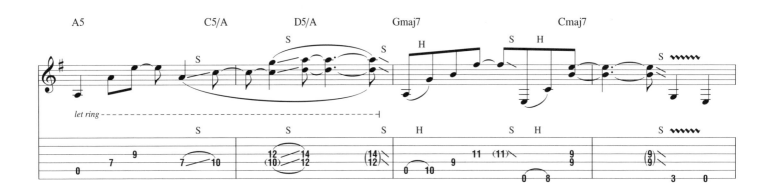

†As before

††Gtr. 2 (clean), Gtr. 3 (dist.); composite arrangement.

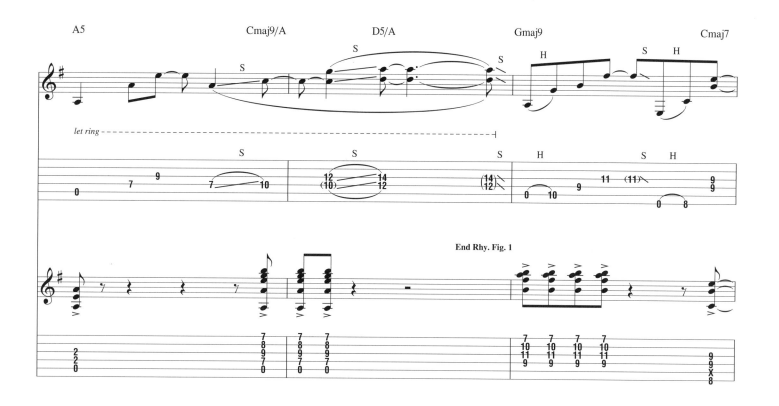

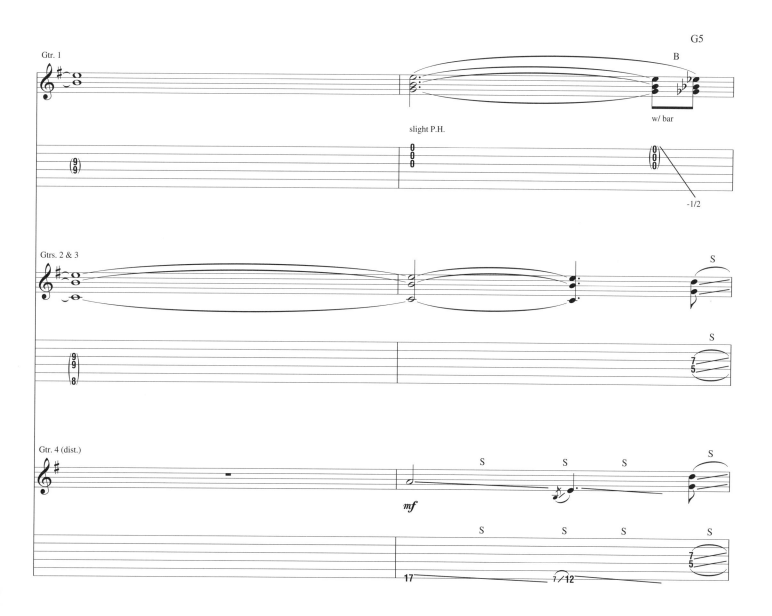

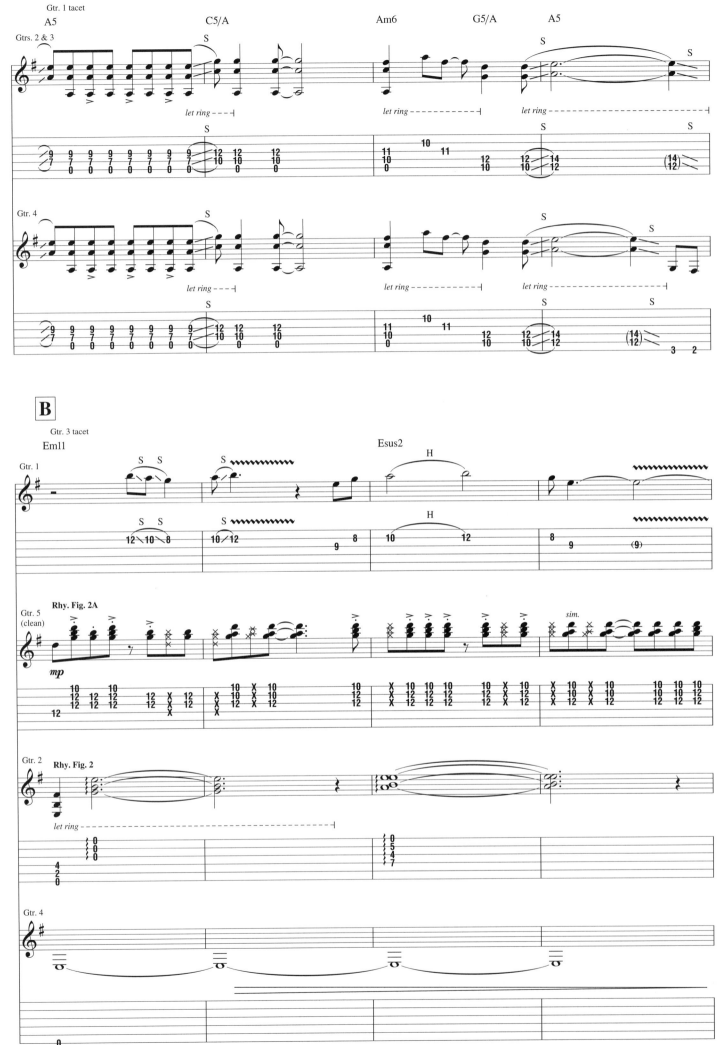

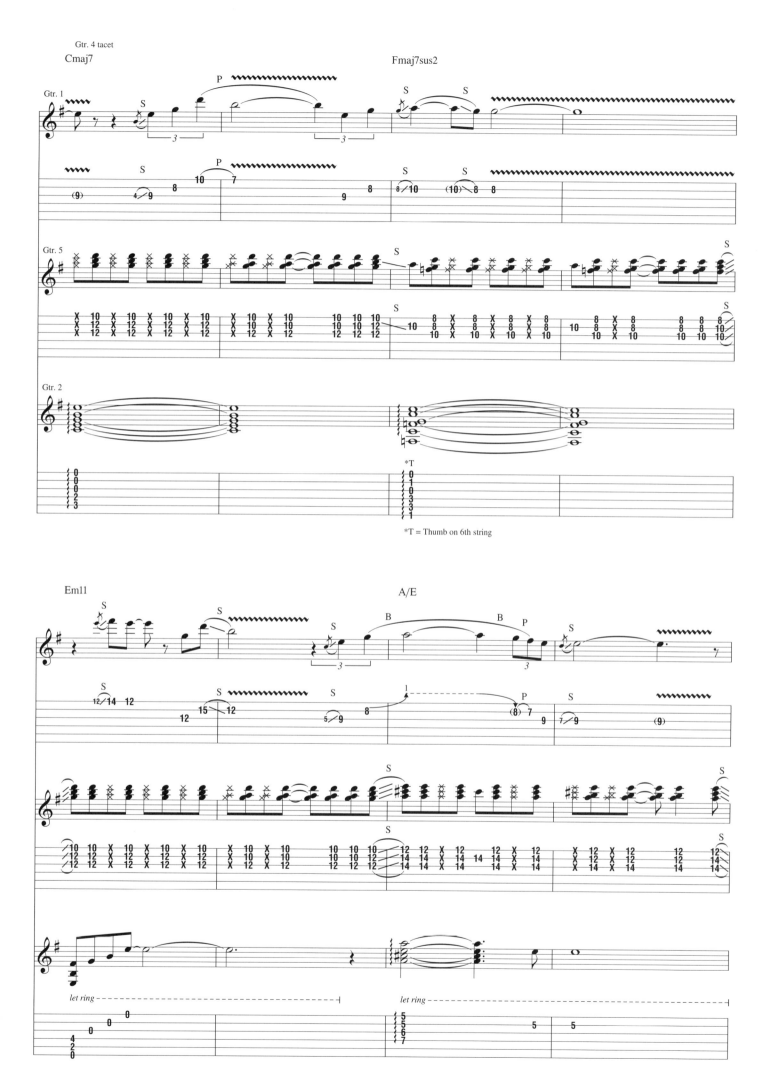

*T = Thumb on 6th string

Cmaj7

Bbmaj7#11

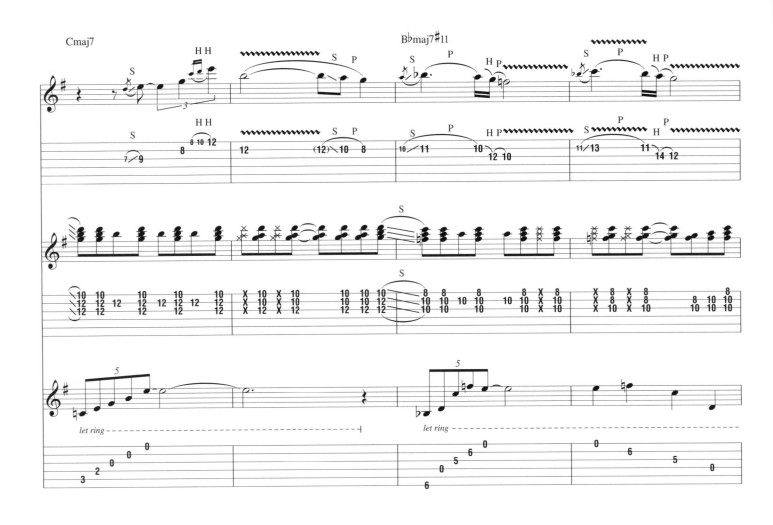

Amaj7

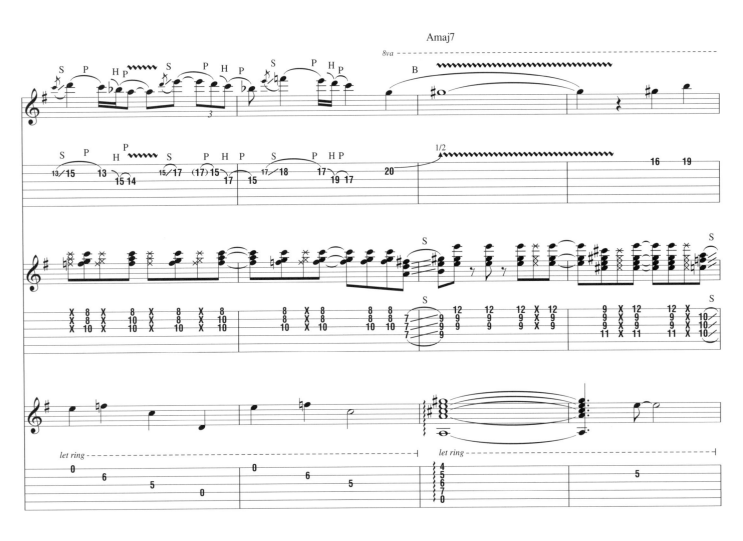

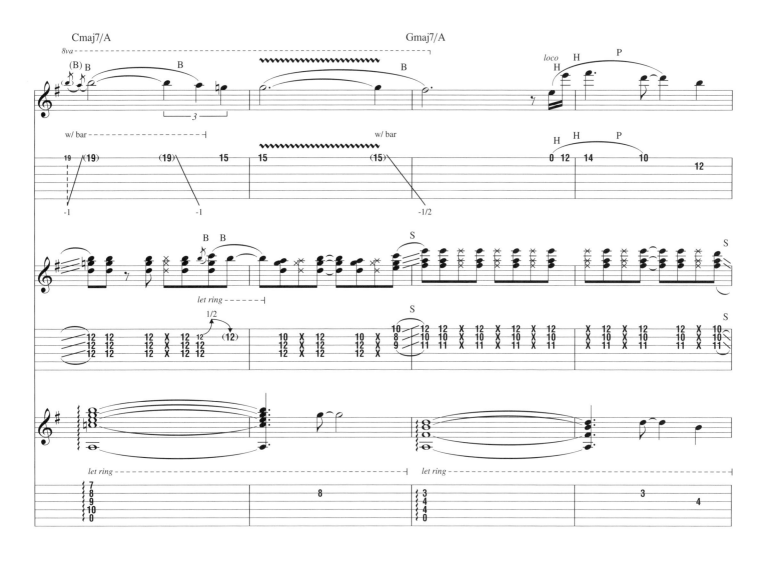

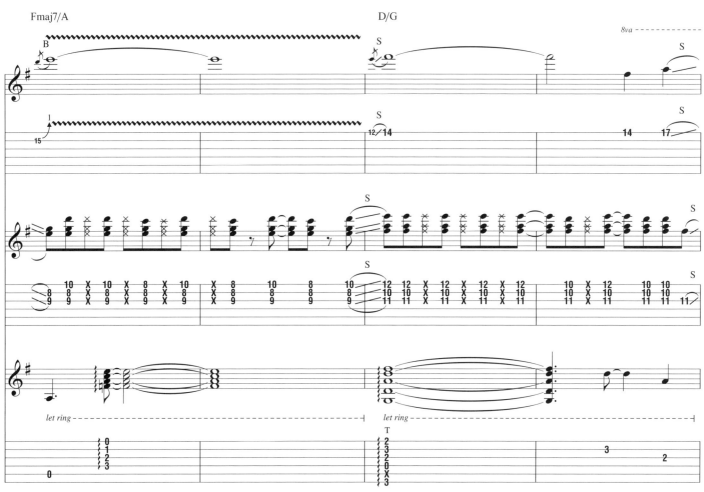

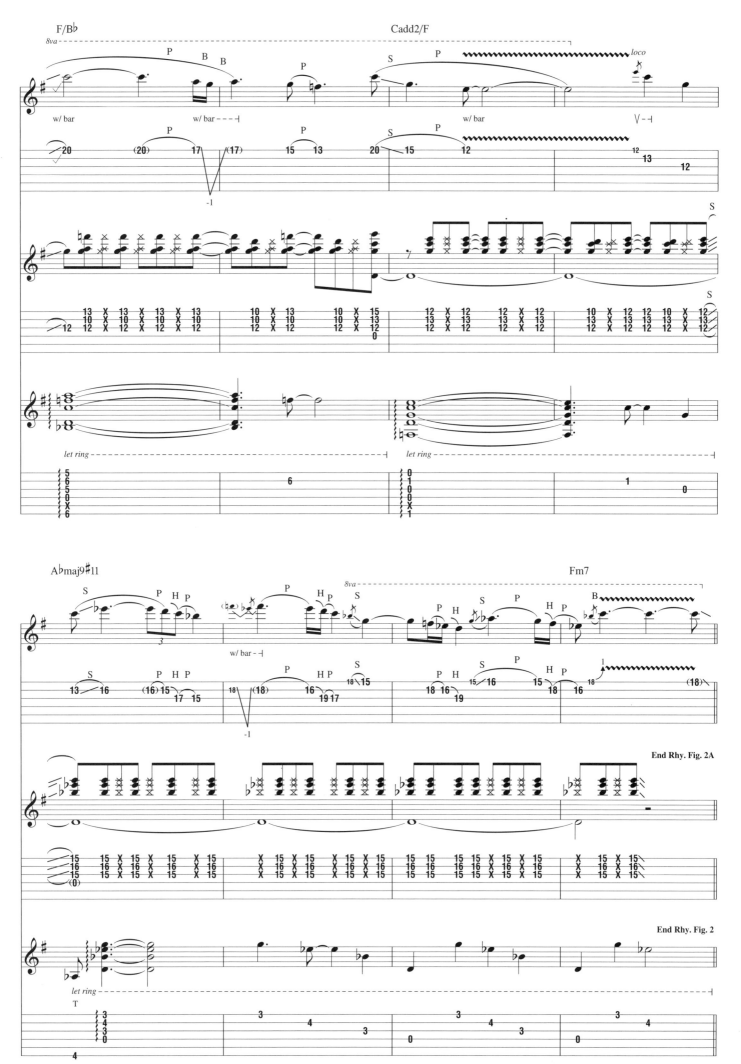

Gtrs. 2 & 3: w/ Rhy. Fig. 1
Gtr. 5 tacet

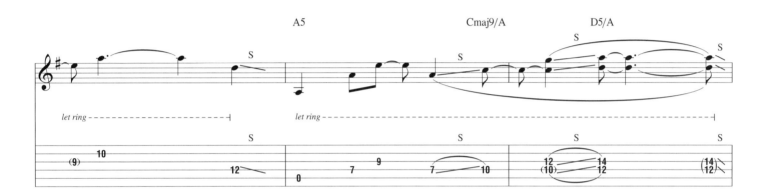

*Key signature denotes A Dorian (next 9 meas.).
**Let open 5th string ring for 6 meas.

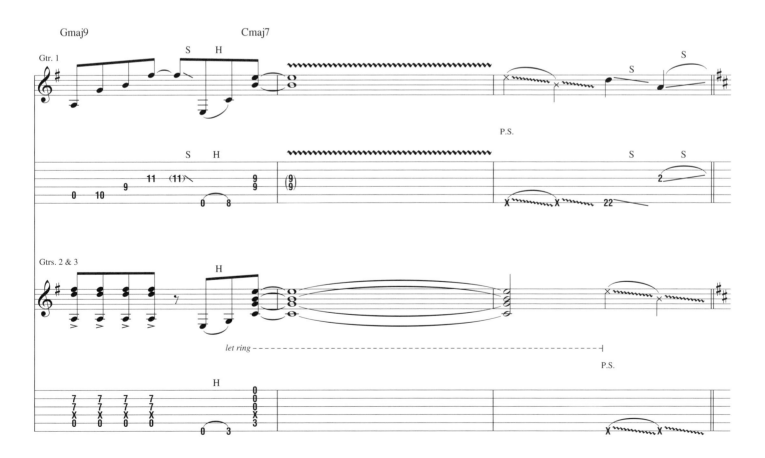

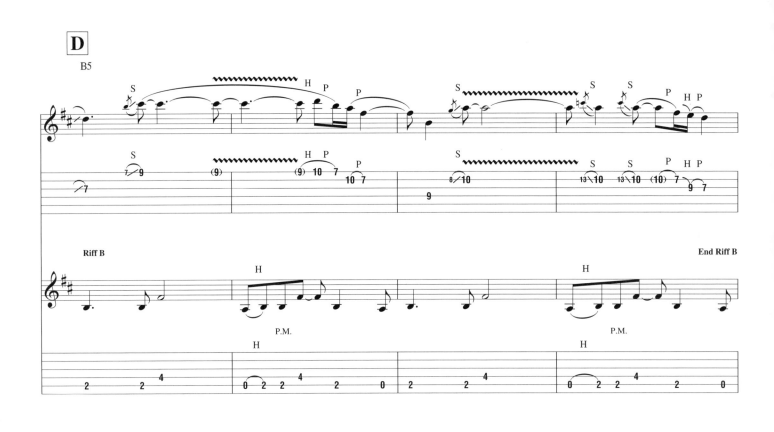

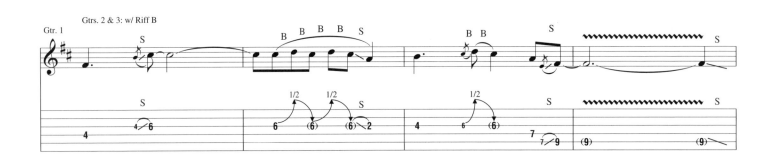

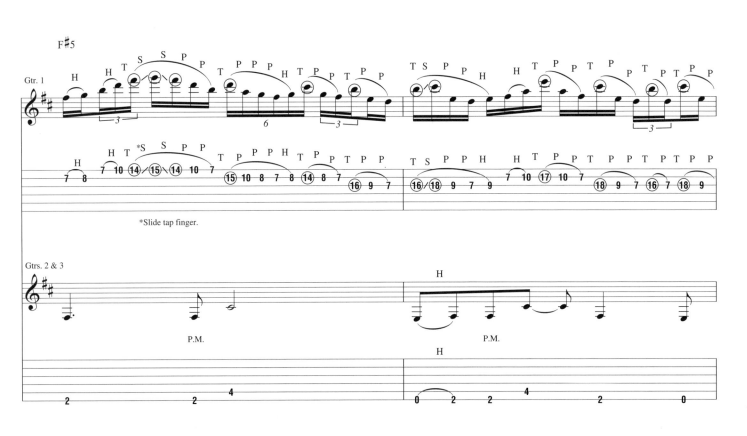

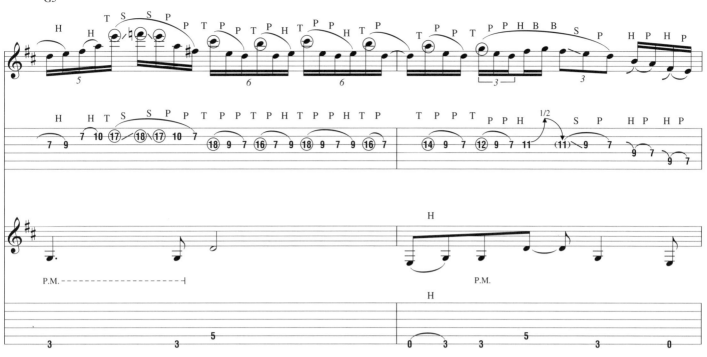

Gtrs. 2 & 3: w/ Riff B

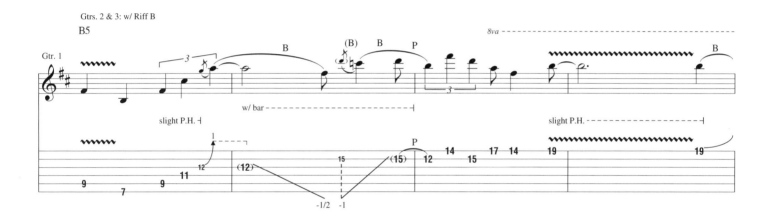

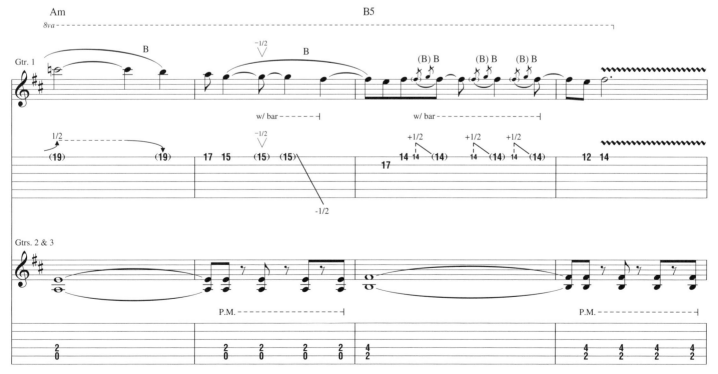

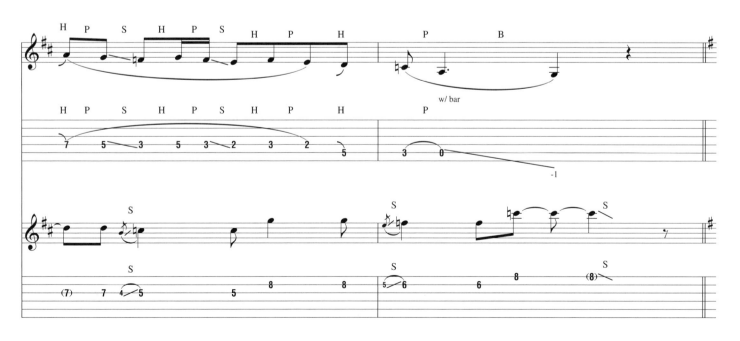

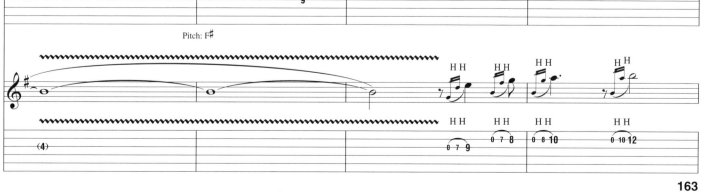

164

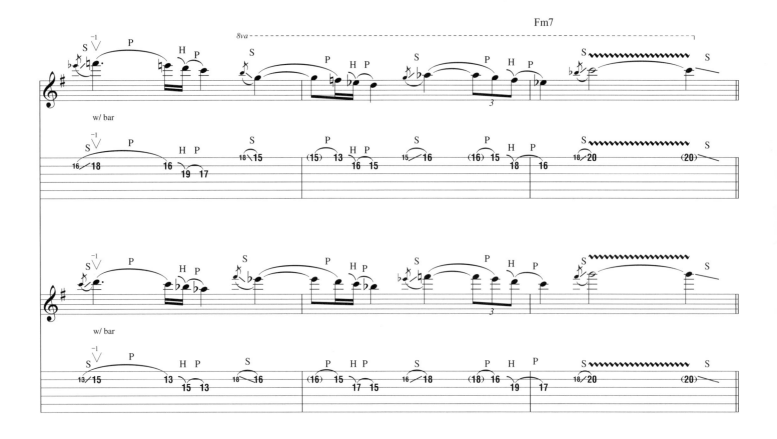

F

Gtr. 1: w/ Riff A
Gtrs. 2 & 3: w/ Rhy. Fig. 1
Gtr. 6 tacet

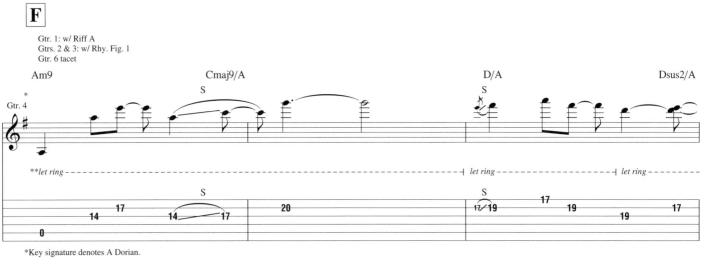

*Key signature denotes A Dorian.
**Let open 5th string ring for 6 meas.

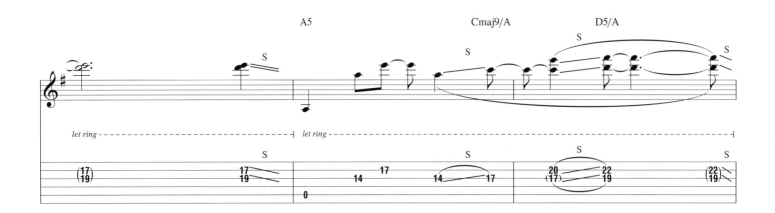

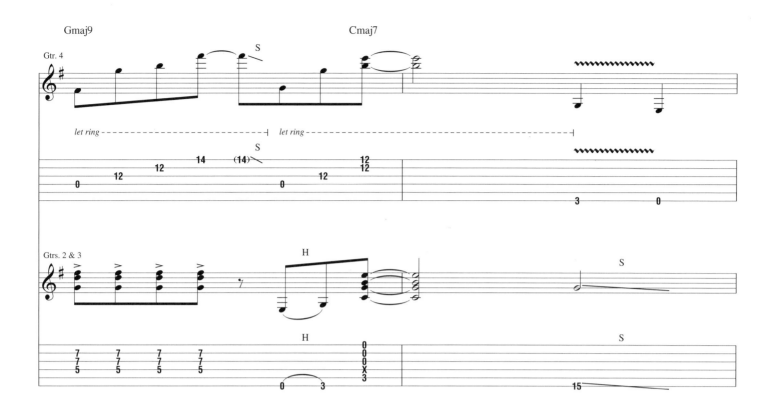

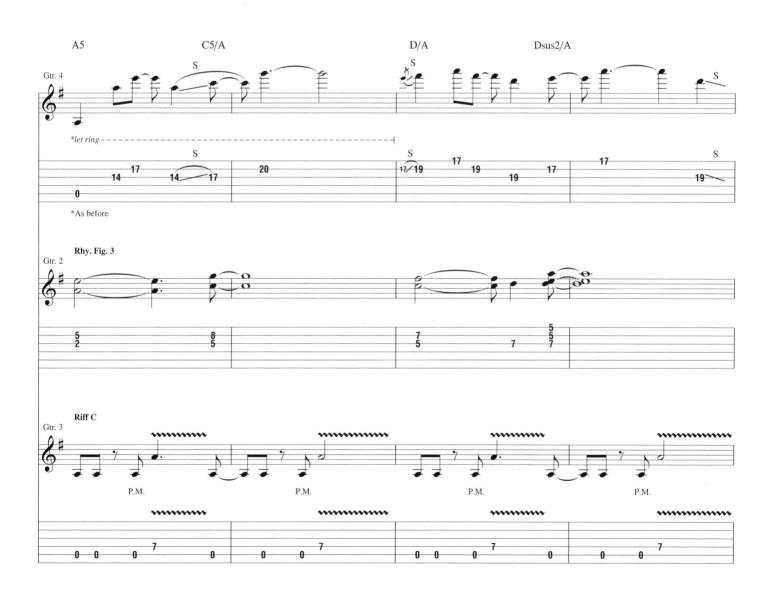

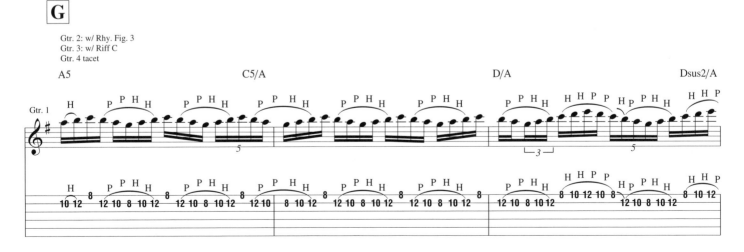

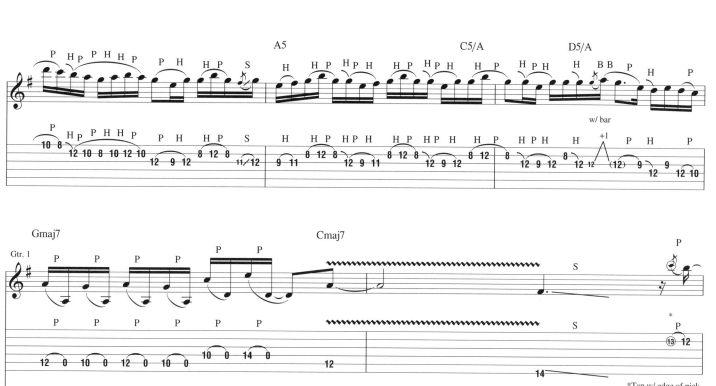

*Tap w/ edge of pick.

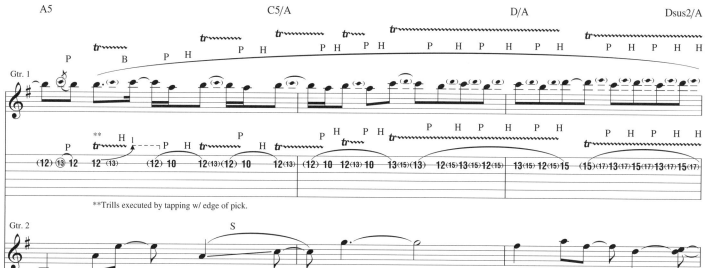

**Trills executed by tapping w/ edge of pick.

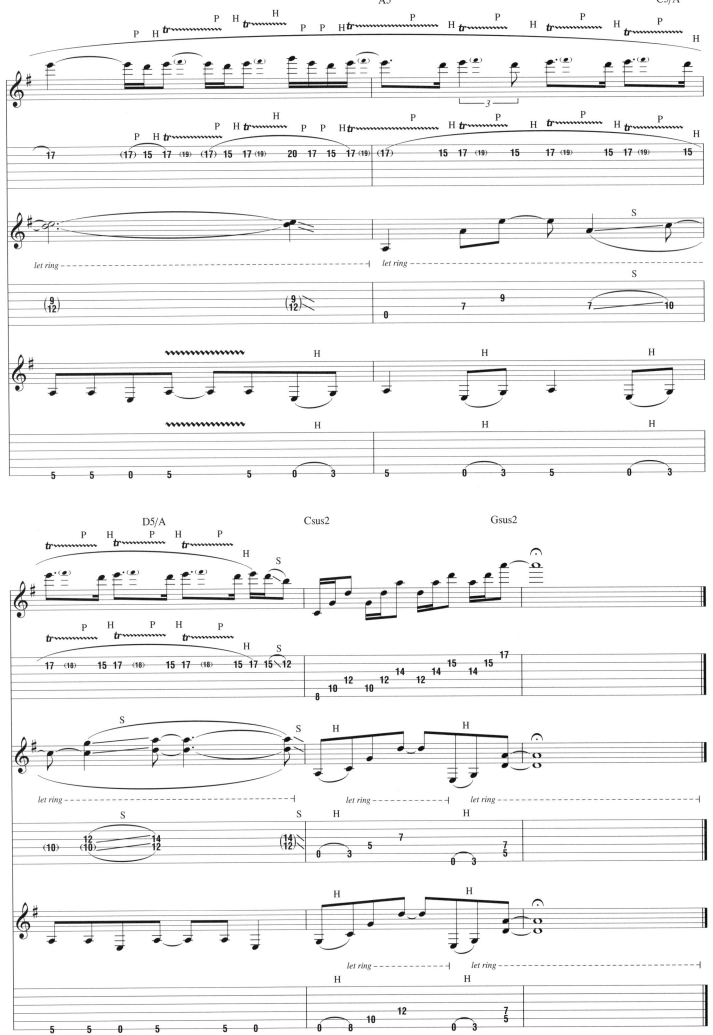

No More Amsterdam

By Steve Vai and Aimee Mann

Gtrs. 1-6: Drop D tuning:
(low to high) D-A-D-G-B-E

Verse
Moderately fast ♩ = 133
Half-time feel

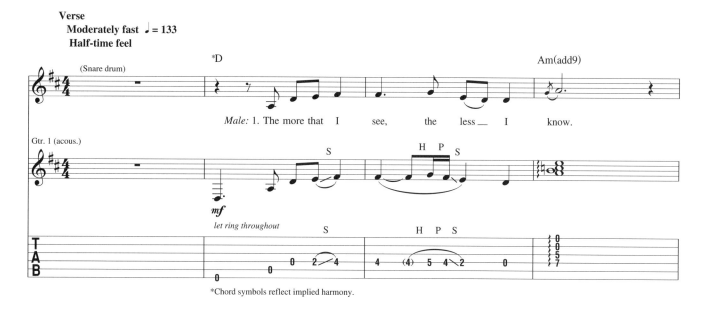

Male: 1. The more that I see, the less __ I know.

Gtr. 1 (acous.)

mf

let ring throughout

*Chord symbols reflect implied harmony.

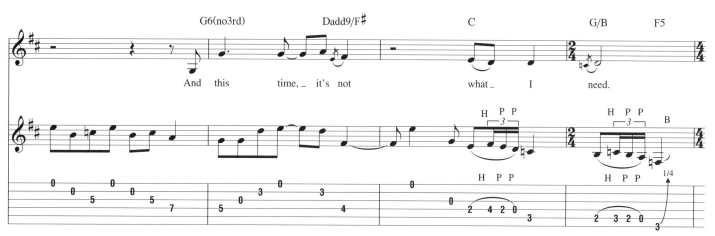

And this time, __ it's not what __ I need.

I wa-ver be-tween go on or just let go, __

Gtr. 1

mf

let ring throughout

Gtr. 2 (acous.)

but hold - ing on is what I'm used to

Gtr. 2 tacet

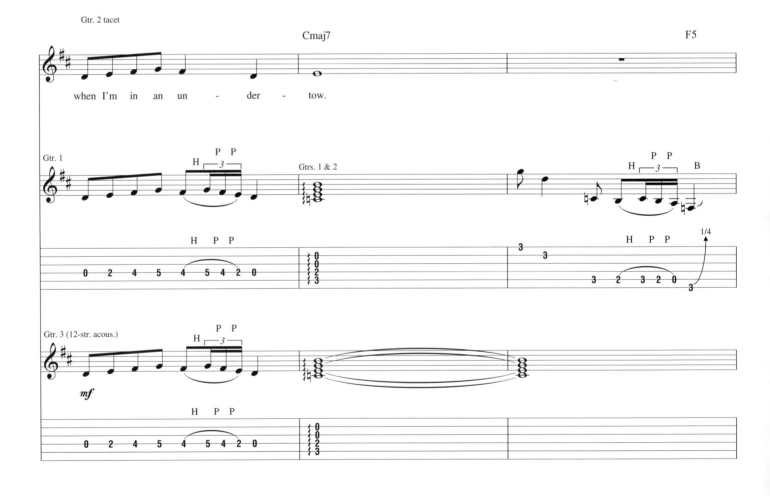

when I'm in an un - der - tow.

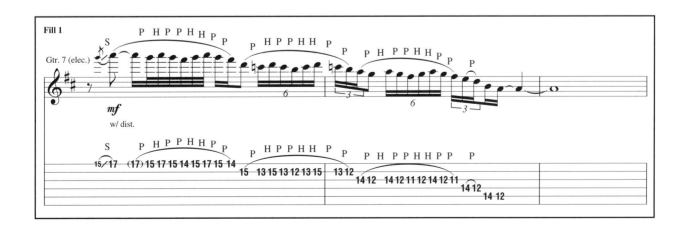

Chorus

Gtr. 5 tacet

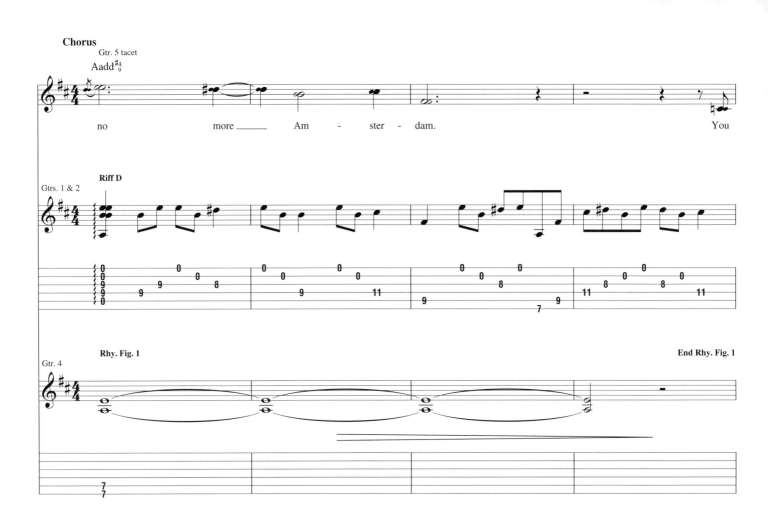

no more _____ Am - ster - dam.   You

made me _____ what I am.   And

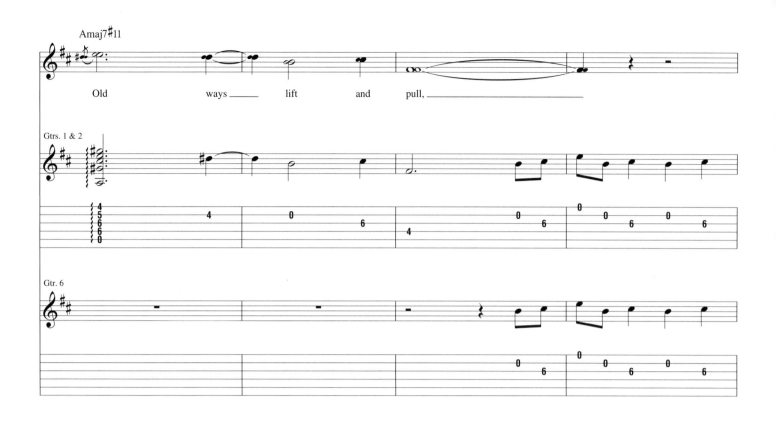

Old ways _____ lift and pull, _____

whole days _____ left half full. _____

Claimed I did - n't mind.

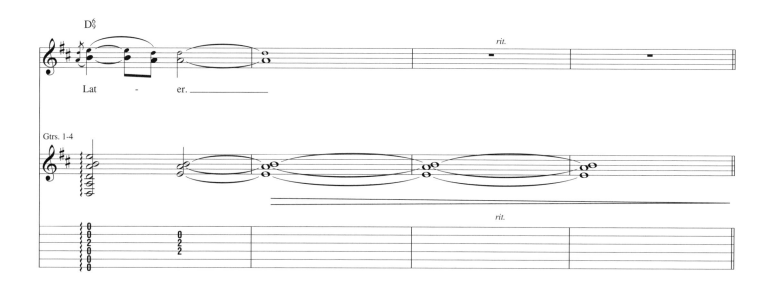

Lat - er.

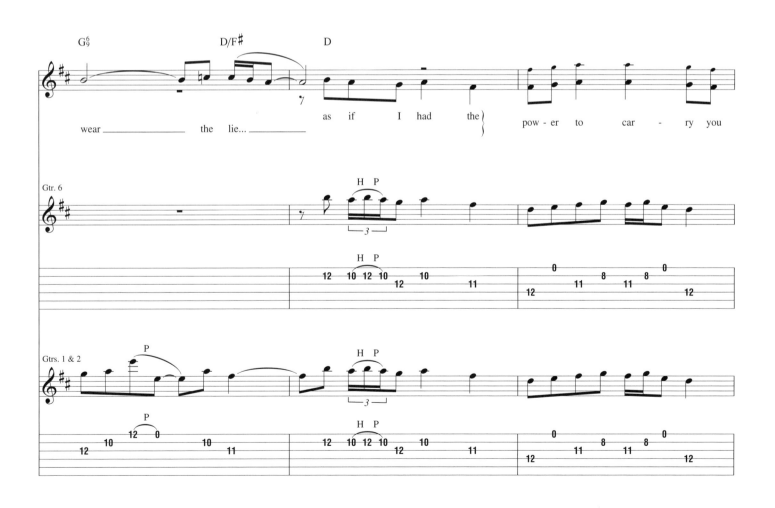

181

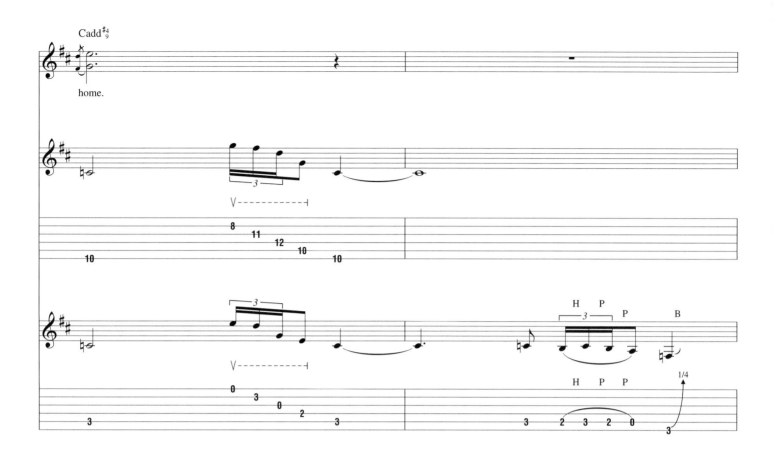

home.

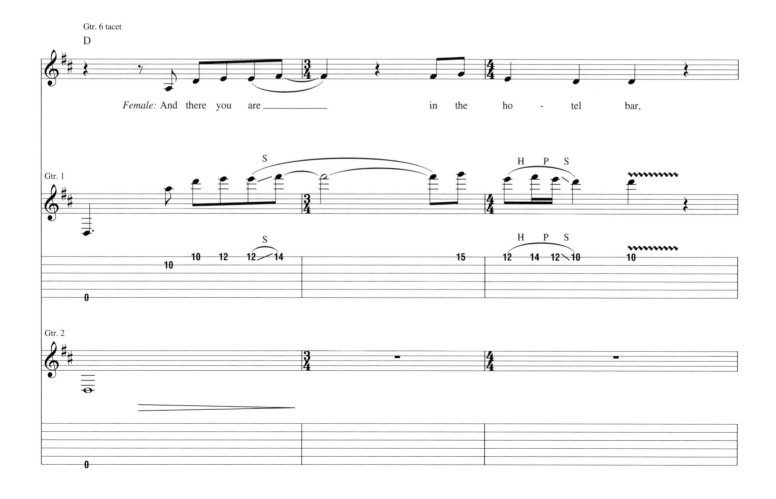

Gtr. 6 tacet

D

Female: And there you are _____ in the ho - tel bar,

Gtr. 1

Gtr. 2

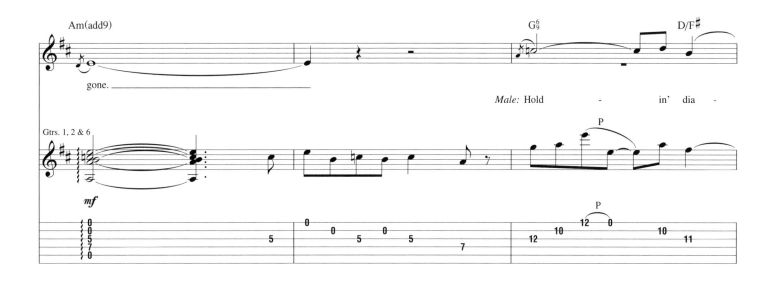

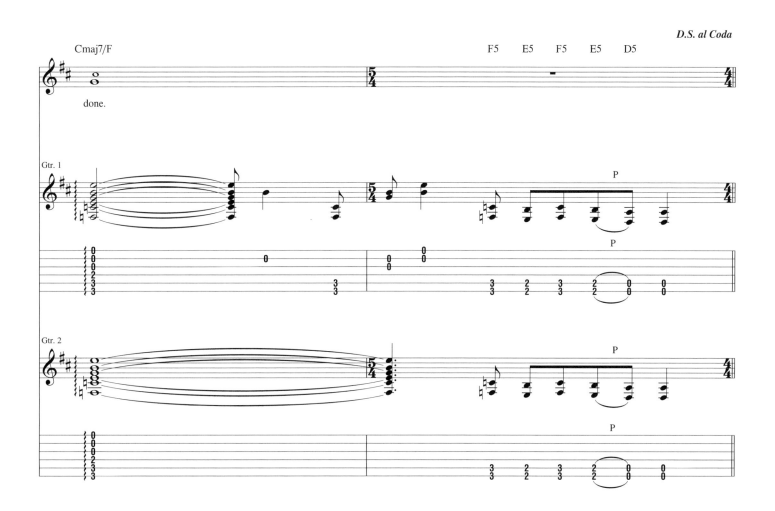

Coda

Chorus

Gtrs. 1 & 2: w/ Riff D
Gtr. 4: w/ Rhy. Fig. 1
Gtr. 5 tacet

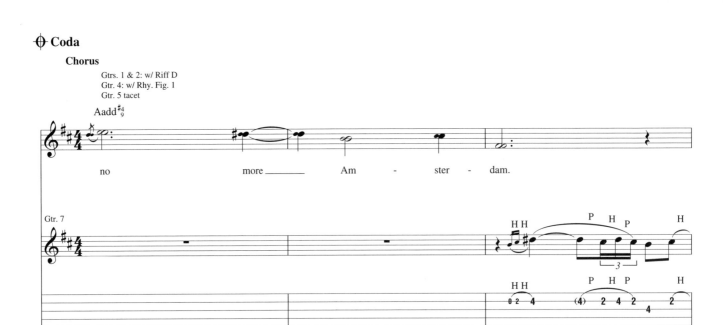

no   more _____ Am - ster - dam.

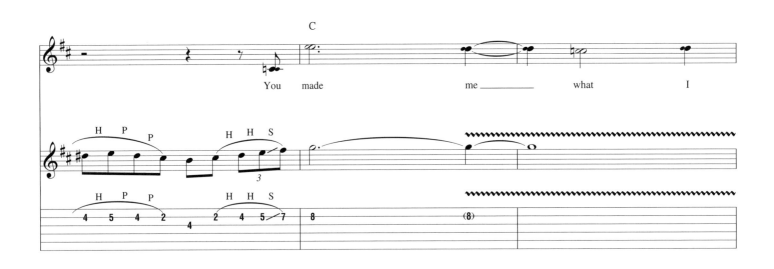

You made   me _____   what   I

Gtr. 6: w/ Riff E

Gtr. 3: w/ Riff F

am.   And   I   can't _____ pay   in

Eadd#4

kind   when some-thing pre - cious al - ways ends   up

Pitch: G

Gtr. 6: w/ Riff G

left   be - hind.

Amaj7#11

Old   ways ___ lift   and   pull,   (And I can't stay hon - est.)

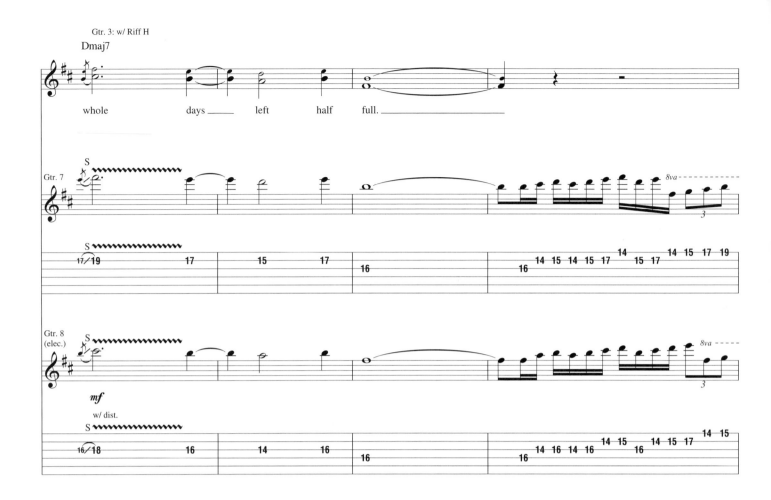

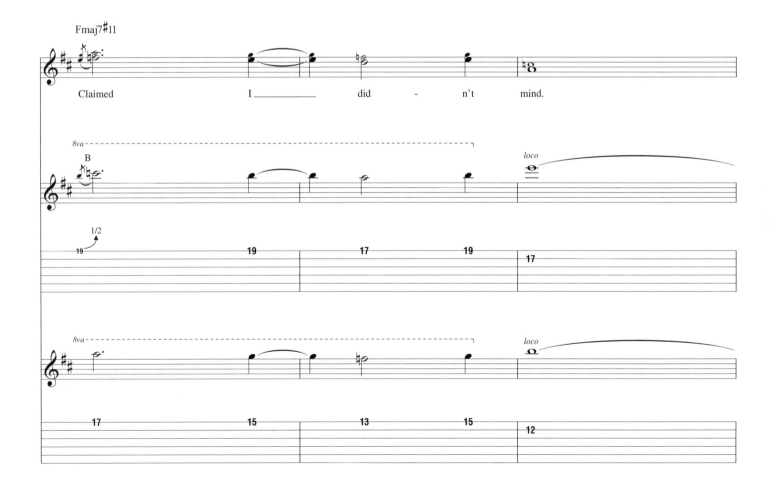

The more that I see, the less __ I know.

Sunshine Electric Raindrops

By Steve Vai

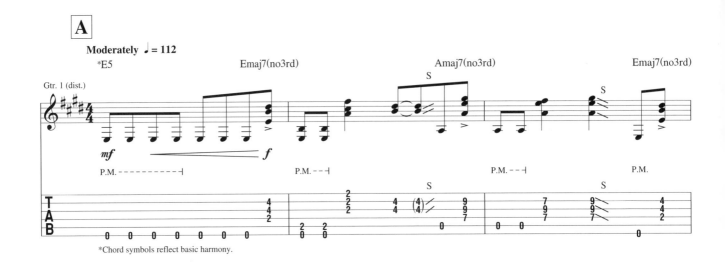

*Chord symbols reflect basic harmony.

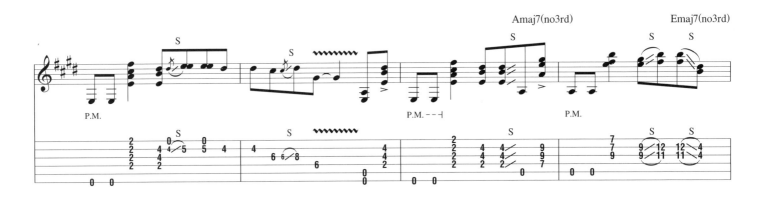

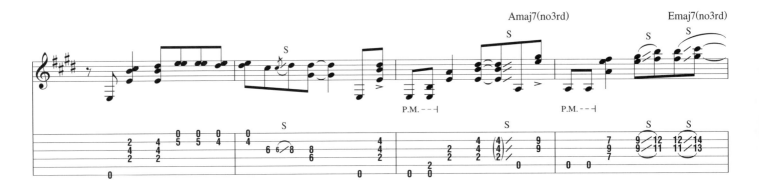

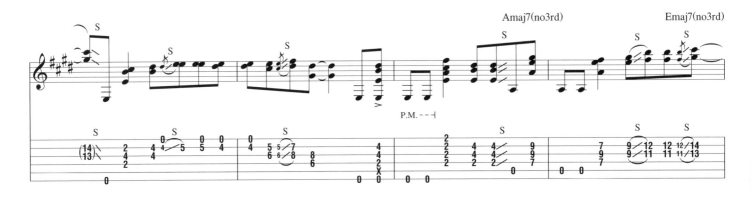

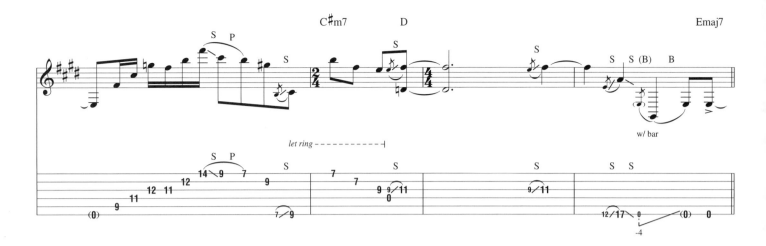

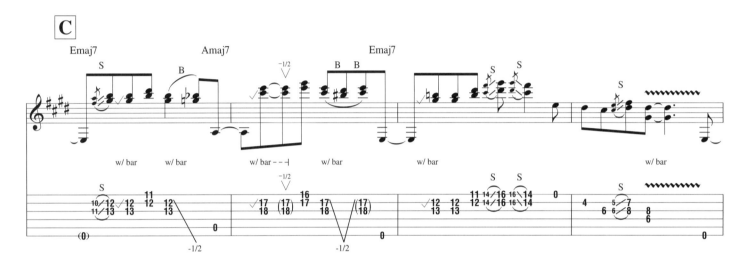

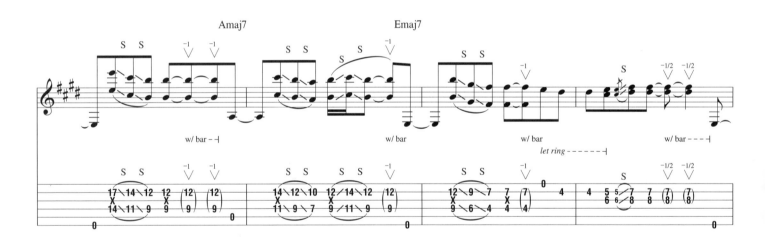

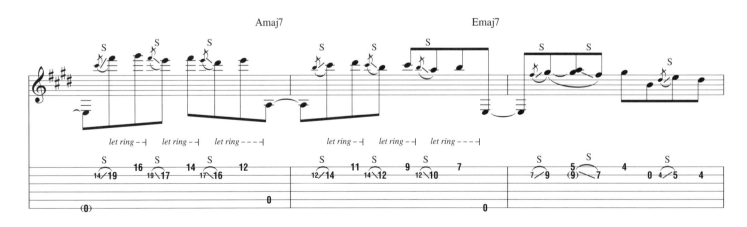

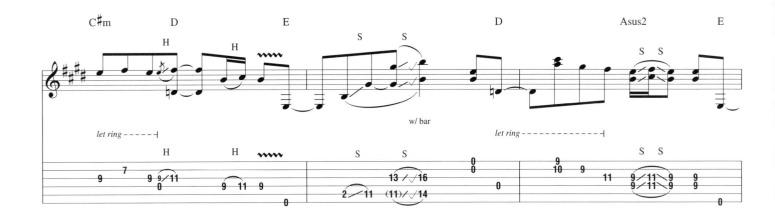

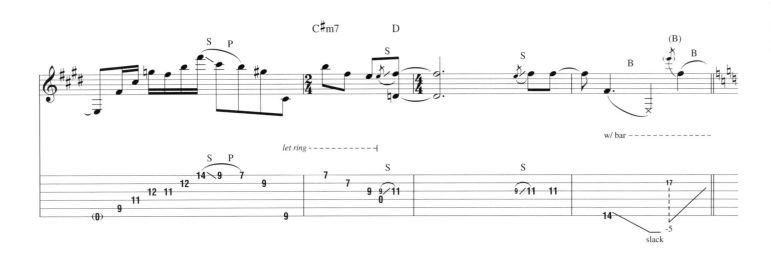

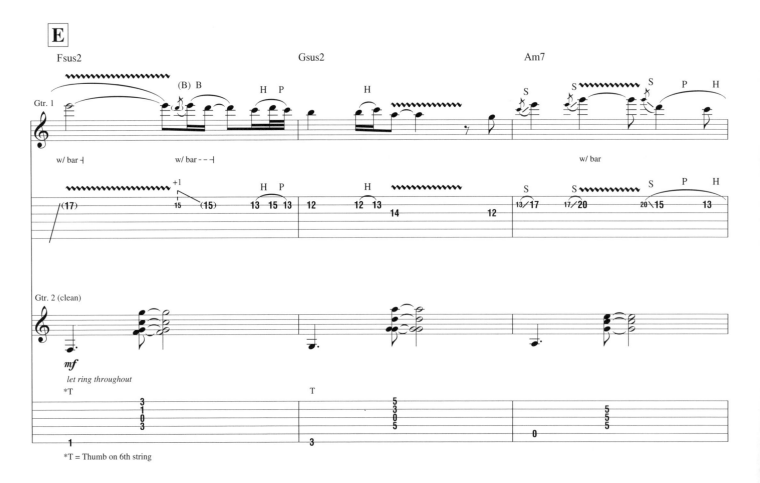

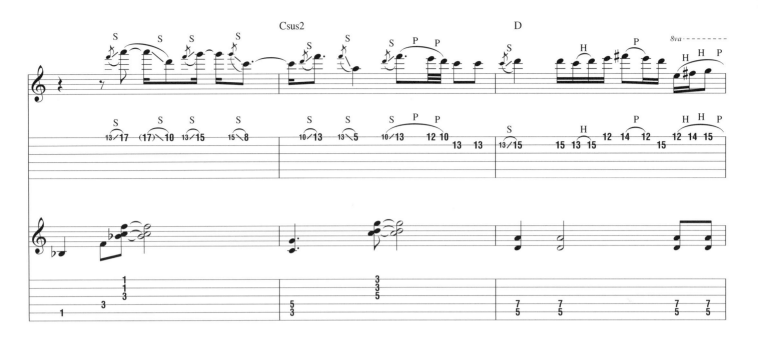

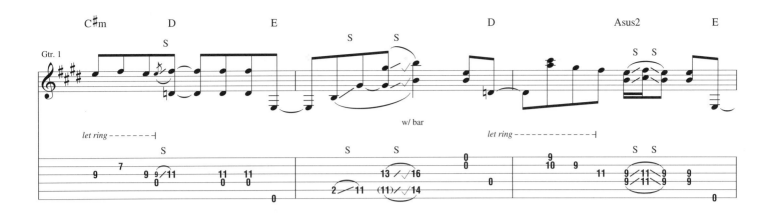

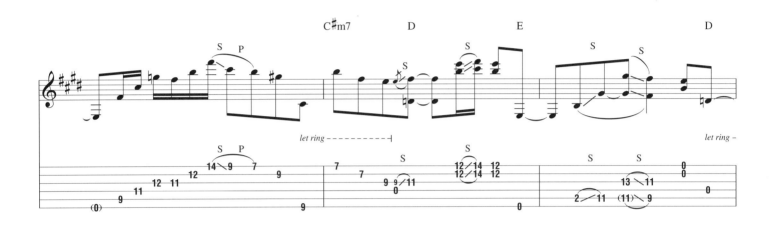

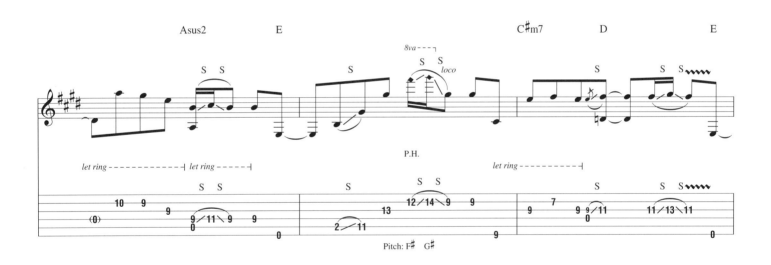

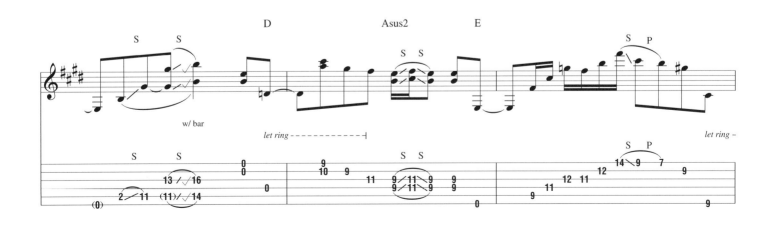

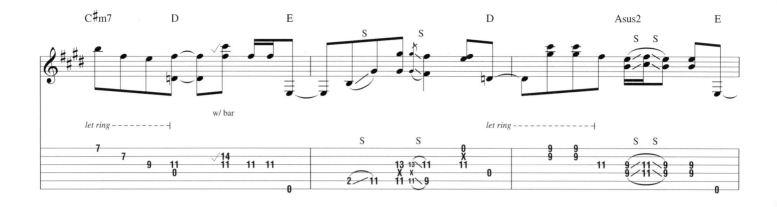

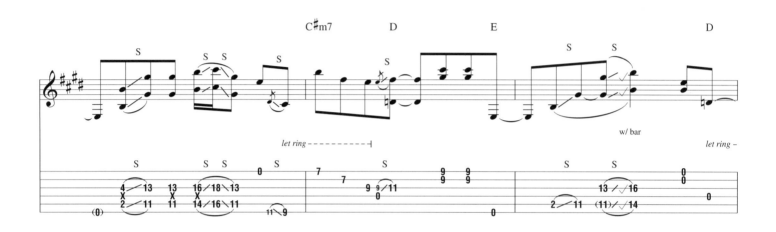

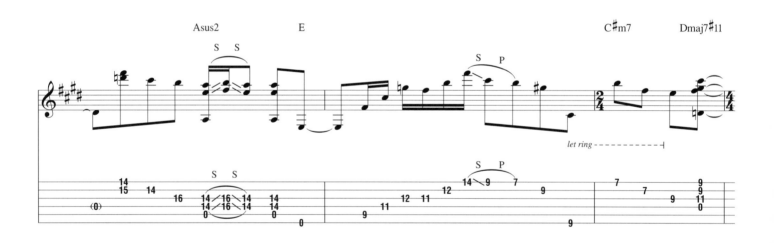

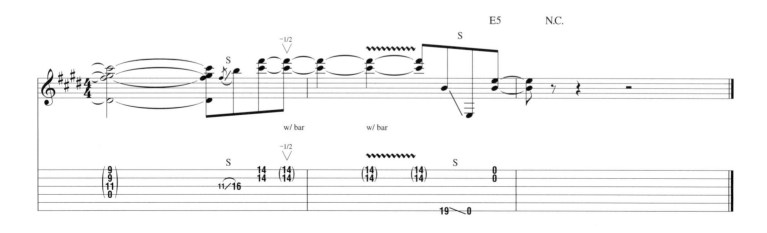

GUITAR NOTATION LEGEND

BEND: Strike note and bend upwards. Numbers over arrows in TAB indicate the number of steps the fretted pitch should be raised.

BEND AND RELEASE: Strike and bend upwards, then release the bend back to the original note. Only the first note is struck.

GRADUAL BEND: Bend up to the specified pitches in the rhythm indicated.

PREBEND: Bend the note upwards, then strike it.

PREBEND AND RELEASE: Bend the note upwards, then strike it and release the bend back to the original note.

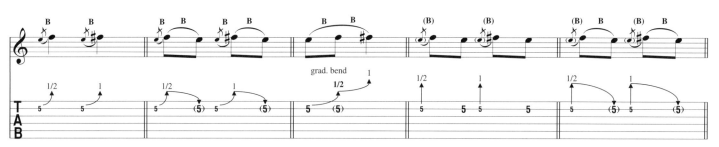

VIBRATO: The string is vibrated by rapidly bending and releasing the note with the left hand or vibrato bar. w/ bar means "with bar."

WIDE OR EXAGGERATED VIBRATO: The pitch is varied to a greater degree by vibrating with the left hand or vibrato bar.

VIBRATO BAR: The pitch of the note or chord is dropped or raised using the vibrato bar.

VIBRATO BAR SCOOP: Depress the bar just before striking the note, then quickly release the bar.

VIBRATO BAR DIP: Strike the note and then immediately drop the specified number of steps, then release back to the original pitch.

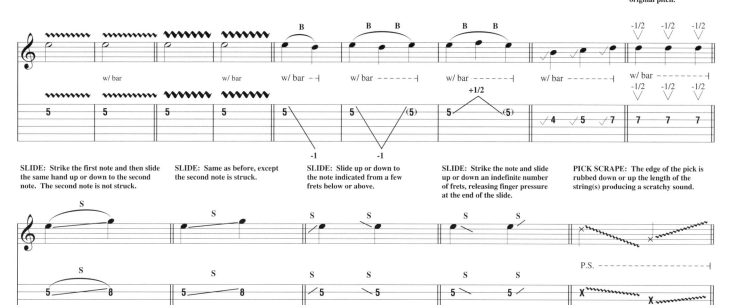

SLIDE: Strike the first note and then slide the same hand up or down to the second note. The second note is not struck.

SLIDE: Same as before, except the second note is struck.

SLIDE: Slide up or down to the note indicated from a few frets below or above.

SLIDE: Strike the note and slide up or down an indefinite number of frets, releasing finger pressure at the end of the slide.

PICK SCRAPE: The edge of the pick is rubbed down or up the length of the string(s) producing a scratchy sound.

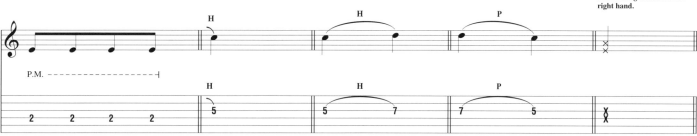

PALM MUTING: The note is muted by lightly touching the string(s) just before the bridge.

HAMMER-ON: Without picking, sound the note by sharply fretting the note with a left-hand finger.

HAMMER-ON: Strike the first (lower) note, then sound the higher note with another finger by fretting it without picking.

PULL-OFF: Place both fingers on the notes to be sounded. Strike the first (higher) note and without picking, pull the finger off to sound the lower note.

MUFFLED STRINGS: A percussive sound is made by laying the left hand across the strings without depressing, and striking them with the right hand.

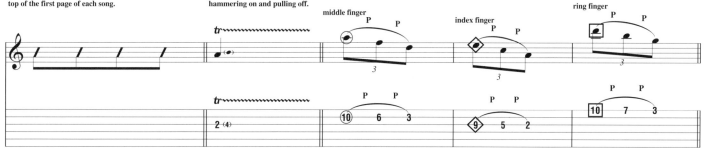

RHYTHM SLASHES: Strum chords in rhythm indicated. Use chord voicings found in the fingering diagrams at the top of the first page of each song.

TRILL: Very rapidly alternate between the 2 notes by hammering on and pulling off.

TAPPING: Hammer (tap) the fret indicated with the appropriate right-hand finger and pull-off to the note(s) indicated with the left-hand.

GUITAR RECORDED VERSIONS®

Guitar Recorded Versions® are note-for-note transcriptions of guitar music taken directly off recordings
This series, one of the most popular in print today, features some of the greatest
guitar players and groups from blues and rock to country and jazz.

Guitar Recorded Versions are transcribed by the best transcribers in the business
Every book contains notes and tablature. Visit www.halleonard.com for our complete selection.

**AUTHENTIC TRANSCRIPTIONS
WITH NOTES AND TABLATURE**

00690898 John 5 – The Devil Knows My Name $22.95
00690959 John 5 – Requiem $22.95
00690814 John 5 – Songs for Sanity $19.95
00690751 John 5 – Vertigo $19.95
00694912 Eric Johnson – Ah Via Musicom $19.95
00690660 Best of Eric Johnson $22.99
00690845 Eric Johnson – Bloom $19.95
00691076 Eric Johnson – Up Close $22.99
00690169 Eric Johnson – Venus Isle $22.95
00690846 Jack Johnson and Friends – Sing-A-Longs and Lullabies for the Film Curious George $19.95
00690271 Robert Johnson – The New Transcriptions $24.95
00699131 Best of Janis Joplin $19.95
00690427 Best of Judas Priest $22.99
00690651 Juanes – Exitos de Juanes $19.95
00690277 Best of Kansas $19.95
00690911 Best of Phil Keaggy $24.99
00690727 Toby Keith Guitar Collection $19.99
00690888 The Killers – Sam's Town $19.95
00690504 Very Best of Albert King $19.95
00690444 B.B. King & Eric Clapton – Riding with the King $22.99
00690134 Freddie King Collection $19.95
00691062 Kings of Leon – Come Around Sundown $22.99
00690975 Kings of Leon – Only by the Night $22.99
00690339 Best of the Kinks $19.95
00690157 Kiss – Alive! $19.95
00690356 Kiss – Alive II $22.99
00694903 Best of Kiss for Guitar $24.95
00690355 Kiss – Destroyer $16.95
14026320 Mark Knopfler – Get Lucky $22.99
00690164 Mark Knopfler Guitar – Vol. 1 $19.95
00690163 Mark Knopfler/Chet Atkins – Neck and Neck $19.95
00690780 Korn – Greatest Hits, Volume 1 $22.95
00690836 Korn – See You on the Other Side $19.95
00690377 Kris Kristofferson Collection $19.95
00690861 Kutless – Hearts of the Innocent $19.95
00690834 Lamb of God – Ashes of the Wake $19.95
00690875 Lamb of God – Sacrament $19.95
00690977 Ray LaMontagne – Gossip in the Grain $19.99
00690890 Ray LaMontagne – Till the Sun Turns Black $19.95
00690823 Ray LaMontagne – Trouble $19.95
00691057 Ray LaMontagne and the Pariah Dogs – God Willin' & The Creek Don't Rise $22.99
00690658 Johnny Lang – Long Time Coming $19.95
00690679 John Lennon – Guitar Collection $19.95
00690781 Linkin Park – Hybrid Theory $22.95
00690782 Linkin Park – Meteora $22.95
00690922 Linkin Park – Minutes to Midnight $19.95
00690783 Best of Live $19.95
00699623 The Best of Chuck Loeb $19.95
00690743 Los Lonely Boys $19.95
00690720 Lostprophets – Start Something $19.95
00690525 Best of George Lynch $24.99
00690955 Lynyrd Skynyrd – All-Time Greatest Hits $19.99
00694954 New Best of Lynyrd Skynyrd $19.95
00690577 Yngwie Malmsteen – Anthology $24.95
00694845 Yngwie Malmsteen – Fire and Ice $19.95
00694757 Yngwie Malmsteen – Trilogy $19.95
00690754 Marilyn Manson – Lest We Forget $19.95
00694956 Bob Marley – Legend $19.95
00690548 Very Best of Bob Marley & The Wailers – One Love $22.99
00694945 Bob Marley – Songs of Freedom $24.95
00690914 Maroon 5 – It Won't Be Soon Before Long $19.95
00690657 Maroon 5 – Songs About Jane $19.95
00690748 Maroon 5 – 1.22.03 Acoustic $19.95
00690989 Mastodon – Crack the Skye $22.99
00691176 Mastodon – The Hunter $22.99
00690442 Matchbox 20 – Mad Season $19.95
00690616 Matchbox Twenty – More Than You Think You Are $19.95
00690239 Matchbox 20 – Yourself or Someone like You $19.95
00691034 Andy McKee – Joyland $19.99
00690382 Sarah McLachlan – Mirrorball $19.95
00120080 The Don McLean Songbook $19.95
00694952 Megadeth – Countdown to Extinction $22.95
00690244 Megadeth – Cryptic Writings $19.95
00694951 Megadeth – Rust in Peace $22.95
00690011 Megadeth – Youthanasia $19.95
00690505 John Mellencamp Guitar Collection $19.95
00690562 Pat Metheny – Bright Size Life $19.95
00691073 Pat Metheny with Christian McBride & Antonion Sanchez – Day Trip/Tokyo Day Trip Live $22.99
00690646 Pat Metheny – One Quiet Night $19.95
00690559 Pat Metheny – Question & Answer $19.95
00690040 Steve Miller Band Greatest Hits $19.95
00690769 Modest Mouse – Good News for People Who Love Bad News $19.95
00102591 Wes Montgomery Guitar Anthology $24.99
00694802 Gary Moore – Still Got the Blues $22.99
00691005 Best of Motion City Soundtrack $19.99
00690787 Mudvayne – L.D. 50 $22.95
00691070 Mumford & Sons – Sigh No More $22.99
00690996 My Morning Jacket Collection $19.99
00690984 Matt Nathanson – Some Mad Hope $22.99
00690611 Nirvana $22.95
00694895 Nirvana – Bleach $19.95
00690189 Nirvana – From the Muddy Banks of the Wishkah $19.95
00694913 Nirvana – In Utero $19.95
00694883 Nirvana – Nevermind $19.95
00690026 Nirvana – Unplugged in New York $19.95
00120112 No Doubt – Tragic Kingdom $22.95
00690226 Oasis – The Other Side of Oasis $19.95
00307163 Oasis – Time Flies... 1994-2009 $19.99
00690358 The Offspring – Americana $19.95
00690203 The Offspring – Smash $18.95
00690818 The Best of Opeth $22.95
00691052 Roy Orbison – Black & White Night $22.99
00694847 Best of Ozzy Osbourne $22.95
00690399 Ozzy Osbourne – The Ozzman Cometh $22.99
00690129 Ozzy Osbourne – Ozzmosis $22.95
00690933 Best of Brad Paisley $22.95
00690995 Brad Paisley – Play: The Guitar Album $24.99
00690866 Panic! At the Disco – A Fever You Can't Sweat Out $19.95
00690939 Christopher Parkening – Solo Pieces $19.99
00690594 Best of Les Paul $19.95
00694855 Pearl Jam – Ten $22.99
00690439 A Perfect Circle – Mer De Noms $19.95
00690661 A Perfect Circle – Thirteenth Step $19.95
00690725 Best of Carl Perkins $19.99
00690499 Tom Petty – Definitive Guitar Collection $19.95
00690868 Tom Petty – Highway Companion $19.95
00690176 Phish – Billy Breathes $22.95
00691249 Phish – Junta $22.99
00690428 Pink Floyd – Dark Side of the Moon $19.95
00690789 Best of Poison $19.95
00693864 Best of The Police $19.95
00690299 Best of Elvis: The King of Rock 'n' Roll $19.95
00692535 Elvis Presley $19.95
00690925 The Very Best of Prince $22.99
00690003 Classic Queen $24.95
00694975 Queen – Greatest Hits $24.95
00690670 Very Best of Queensryche $19.95
00690878 The Raconteurs – Broken Boy Soldiers $19.95
00694910 Rage Against the Machine $19.95
00690179 Rancid – And Out Come the Wolves $22.95
00690426 Best of Ratt $19.95
00690055 Red Hot Chili Peppers – Blood Sugar Sex Magik $19.95
00690584 Red Hot Chili Peppers – By the Way $19.95
00690379 Red Hot Chili Peppers – Californication $19.95
00690673 Red Hot Chili Peppers – Greatest Hits $19.95
00690090 Red Hot Chili Peppers – One Hot Minute $22.95
00691166 Red Hot Chili Peppers – I'm with You $22.99
00690852 Red Hot Chili Peppers – Stadium Arcadium $24.95
00690893 The Red Jumpsuit Apparatus – Don't You Fake It $19.95
00690511 Django Reinhardt – The Definitive Collection $19.95
00690779 Relient K – MMHMM $19.95
00690643 Relient K – Two Lefts Don't Make a Right ... But Three Do $19.95
00690260 Jimmie Rodgers Guitar Collection $19.95
14041901 Rodrigo Y Gabriela and C.U.B.A. – Area 52 $24.99
00690014 Rolling Stones – Exile on Main Street $24.95
00690631 Rolling Stones – Guitar Anthology $27.95
00690685 David Lee Roth – Eat 'Em and Smile $19.95
00690031 Santana's Greatest Hits $19.95
00690796 Very Best of Michael Schenker $19.95
00690566 Best of Scorpions $22.95
00690604 Bob Seger – Guitar Anthology $19.95
00690659 Bob Seger and the Silver Bullet Band – Greatest Hits, Volume 2 $17.95
00691012 Shadows Fall – Retribution $22.99
00690896 Shadows Fall – Threads of Life $19.95
00690803 Best of Kenny Wayne Shepherd Band $19.95
00690750 Kenny Wayne Shepherd – The Place You're In $19.95
00690857 Shinedown – Us and Them $19.95
00690196 Silverchair – Freak Show $19.95
00690130 Silverchair – Frogstomp $19.95
00690872 Slayer – Christ Illusion $19.95
00690813 Slayer – Guitar Collection $19.95
00690419 Slipknot $19.95
00690973 Slipknot – All Hope Is Gone $22.99
00690733 Slipknot – Volume 3 (The Subliminal Verses) $22.99
00690330 Social Distortion – Live at the Roxy $19.95
00120004 Best of Steely Dan $24.95
00694921 Best of Steppenwolf $22.95
00690655 Best of Mike Stern $19.95

RECORDED VERSIONS GUITAR®

AUTHENTIC TRANSCRIPTIONS WITH NOTES AND TABLATURE

00690949 Rod Stewart Guitar Anthology $19.99
00690021 Sting – Fields of Gold $19.95
00690689 Story of the Year – Page Avenue $19.95
00690520 Styx Guitar Collection $19.95
00120081 Sublime $19.95
00690992 Sublime – Robbin' the Hood $19.99
00690519 SUM 41 – All Killer No Filler $19.95
00691072 Best of Supertramp $22.99
00690994 Taylor Swift $22.99
00690993 Taylor Swift – Fearless $22.99
00691063 Taylor Swift – Speak Now $22.99
00690767 Switchfoot – The Beautiful Letdown $19.95
00690830 System of a Down – Hypnotize $19.95
00690531 System of a Down – Toxicity $19.95
00694824 Best of James Taylor $16.95
00694887 Best of Thin Lizzy $19.95
00690871 Three Days Grace – One-X $19.95
00690891 30 Seconds to Mars – A Beautiful Lie $19.95
00690030 Toad the Wet Sprocket $19.95
00690233 The Merle Travis Collection $19.99
00690683 Robin Trower – Bridge of Sighs $19.95
00699191 U2 – Best of: 1980-1990 $19.95
00690732 U2 – Best of: 1990-2000 $19.95
00690894 U2 – 18 Singles $19.95
00690775 U2 – How to Dismantle an Atomic Bomb $22.95
00690997 U2 – No Line on the Horizon $19.99
00690039 Steve Vai – Alien Love Secrets $24.95
00690172 Steve Vai – Fire Garden $24.95
00660137 Steve Vai – Passion & Warfare $24.95
00690881 Steve Vai – Real Illusions: Reflections $24.95
00694904 Steve Vai – Sex and Religion $24.95
00690392 Steve Vai – The Ultra Zone $19.95
00690024 Stevie Ray Vaughan – Couldn't Stand the Weather $19.95
00690370 Stevie Ray Vaughan and Double Trouble – The Real Deal: Greatest Hits Volume 2 $22.95
00690116 Stevie Ray Vaughan – Guitar Collection $24.95
00660136 Stevie Ray Vaughan – In Step $19.95
00694879 Stevie Ray Vaughan – In the Beginning $19.95
00660058 Stevie Ray Vaughan – Lightnin' Blues '83-'87 $24.95
00690036 Stevie Ray Vaughan – Live Alive $24.95
00694835 Stevie Ray Vaughan – The Sky Is Crying $22.95
00690025 Stevie Ray Vaughan – Soul to Soul $19.95
00690015 Stevie Ray Vaughan – Texas Flood $19.95
00690772 Velvet Revolver – Contraband $22.95
00690132 The T-Bone Walker Collection $19.95
00694789 Muddy Waters – Deep Blues $24.95
00690071 Weezer (The Blue Album) $19.95
00690516 Weezer (The Green Album) $19.95
00690286 Weezer – Pinkerton $19.95
00691046 Weezer – Rarities Edition $22.99
00690447 Best of the Who $24.95
00694970 The Who – Definitive Guitar Collection: A-E $24.95
00694971 The Who – Definitive Guitar Collection F-Li $24.95
00694972 The Who – Definitive Guitar Collection: Lo-R $24.95
00690672 Best of Dar Williams $19.95
00691017 Wolfmother – Cosmic Egg $22.99
00690319 Stevie Wonder – Some of the Best $17.95
00690596 Best of the Yardbirds $19.95
00690844 Yellowcard – Lights and Sounds $19.95
00690916 The Best of Dwight Yoakam $19.95
00690904 Neil Young – Harvest $29.99
00690905 Neil Young – Rust Never Sleeps $19.99
00690443 Frank Zappa – Hot Rats $19.95
00690624 Frank Zappa and the Mothers of Invention – One Size Fits All $22.99
00690623 Frank Zappa – Over-Nite Sensation $22.99
00690589 ZZ Top – Guitar Anthology $24.95
00690960 ZZ Top Guitar Classics $19.99

HAL•LEONARD® CORPORATION
7777 W. Bluemound Rd. P.O. Box 13819 Milwaukee, WI 53213

Complete songlists and more at **www.halleonard.com**
Prices, contents, and availability subject to change without notice.

1112

GUITAR *signature licks*

Signature Licks book/CD packs provide a step-by-step breakdown of "right from the record" riffs, licks, and solos so you can jam along with your favorite bands. They contain performance notes and an overview of each artist's or group's style, with note-for-note transcriptions in notes and tab. The CDs feature full-band demos at both normal and slow speeds.

AC/DC
14041352 ....$22.99

ACOUSTIC CLASSICS
00695864 ....$19.95

AEROSMITH 1973-1979
00695106 ....$22.95

AEROSMITH 1979-1998
00695219 ....$22.95

BEST OF AGGRO-METAL
00695592 ....$19.95

DUANE ALLMAN
00696042 ....$22.99

BEST OF CHET ATKINS
00695752 ....$22.95

AVENGED SEVENFOLD
00696473 ....$22.99

THE BEACH BOYS DEFINITIVE COLLECTION
00695683 ....$22.95

BEST OF THE BEATLES FOR ACOUSTIC GUITAR
00695453 ....$22.95

THE BEATLES BASS
00695283 ....$22.95

THE BEATLES FAVORITES
00695096 ....$24.95

THE BEATLES HITS
00695049 ....$24.95

JEFF BECK
00696427 ....$22.99

BEST OF GEORGE BENSON
00695418 ....$22.95

BEST OF BLACK SABBATH
00695249 ....$22.95

BLUES BREAKERS WITH JOHN MAYALL & ERIC CLAPTON
00696374 ....$22.99

BLUES/ROCK GUITAR HEROES
00696381 ....$19.99

BON JOVI
00696380 ....$22.99

KENNY BURRELL
00695830 ....$22.99

BEST OF CHARLIE CHRISTIAN
00695584 ....$22.95

BEST OF ERIC CLAPTON
00695038 ....$24.95

ERIC CLAPTON – FROM THE ALBUM UNPLUGGED
00695250 ....$24.95

BEST OF CREAM
00695251 ....$22.95

CREEDANCE CLEARWATER REVIVAL
00695924 ....$22.95

DEEP PURPLE – GREATEST HITS
00695625 ....$22.95

THE BEST OF DEF LEPPARD
00696516 ....$22.95

THE DOORS
00695373 ....$22.95

TOMMY EMMANUEL
00696409 ....$22.99

ESSENTIAL JAZZ GUITAR
00695875 ....$19.99

FAMOUS ROCK GUITAR SOLOS
00695590 ....$19.95

FLEETWOOD MAC
00696416 ....$22.99

BEST OF FOO FIGHTERS
00695481 ....$24.95

ROBBEN FORD
00695903 ....$22.95

BEST OF GRANT GREEN
00695747 ....$22.95

BEST OF GUNS N' ROSES
00695183 ....$24.95

THE BEST OF BUDDY GUY
00695186 ....$22.99

JIM HALL
00695848 ....$22.99

HARD ROCK SOLOS
00695591 ....$19.95

JIMI HENDRIX
00696560 ....$24.95

JIMI HENDRIX – VOLUME 2
00695835 ....$24.95

JOHN LEE HOOKER
00695894 ....$19.99

HOT COUNTRY GUITAR
00695580 ....$19.95

BEST OF JAZZ GUITAR
00695586 ....$24.95

ERIC JOHNSON
00699317 ....$24.95

ROBERT JOHNSON
00695264 ....$22.95

BARNEY KESSEL
00696009 ....$22.99

THE ESSENTIAL ALBERT KING
00695713 ....$22.95

B.B. KING – BLUES LEGEND
00696039 ....$22.99

B.B. KING – THE DEFINITIVE COLLECTION
00695635 ....$22.95

B.B. KING – MASTER BLUESMAN
00699923 ....$24.99

THE KINKS
00695553 ....$22.95

BEST OF KISS
00699413 ....$22.95

MARK KNOPFLER
00695178 ....$22.95

LYNYRD SKYNYRD
00695872 ....$24.95

THE BEST OF YNGWIE MALMSTEEN
00695669 ....$22.95

BEST OF PAT MARTINO
00695632 ....$24.99

MEGADETH
00696421 ....$22.99

WES MONTGOMERY
00695387 ....$24.95

BEST OF NIRVANA
00695483 ....$24.95

THE OFFSPRING
00695852 ....$24.95

VERY BEST OF OZZY OSBOURNE
00695431 ....$22.95

BRAD PAISLEY
00696379 ....$22.99

BEST OF JOE PASS
00695730 ....$22.95

JACO PASTORIUS
00695544 ....$24.95

TOM PETTY
00696021 ....$22.99

PINK FLOYD – EARLY CLASSICS
00695566 ....$22.95

THE GUITARS OF ELVIS
00696507 ....$22.95

BEST OF QUEEN
00695097 ....$24.95

BEST OF RAGE AGAINST THE MACHINE
00695480 ....$24.95

RED HOT CHILI PEPPERS
00695173 ....$22.95

RED HOT CHILI PEPPERS – GREATEST HITS
00695828 ....$24.95

BEST OF DJANGO REINHARDT
00695660 ....$24.95

BEST OF ROCK
00695884 ....$19.95

BEST OF ROCK 'N' ROLL GUITAR
00695559 ....$19.95

BEST OF ROCKABILLY GUITAR
00695785 ....$19.95

THE ROLLING STONES
00695079 ....$24.95

BEST OF DAVID LEE ROTH
00695843 ....$24.95

BEST OF JOE SATRIANI
00695216 ....$22.95

BEST OF SILVERCHAIR
00695488 ....$22.95

THE BEST OF SOUL GUITAR
00695703 ....$19.95

BEST OF SOUTHERN ROCK
00695560 ....$19.95

STEELY DAN
00696015 ....$22.99

MIKE STERN
00695800 ....$24.99

BEST OF SURF GUITAR
00695822 ....$19.95

BEST OF SYSTEM OF A DOWN
00695788 ....$22.95

ROBIN TROWER
00695950 ....$22.95

STEVE VAI
00673247 ....$22.95

STEVE VAI – ALIEN LOVE SECRETS: THE NAKED VAMPS
00695223 ....$22.95

STEVE VAI – FIRE GARDEN: THE NAKED VAMPS
00695166 ....$22.95

STEVE VAI – THE ULTRA ZONE: NAKED VAMPS
00695684 ....$22.95

STEVIE RAY VAUGHAN – 2ND ED.
00699316 ....$24.95

THE GUITAR STYLE OF STEVIE RAY VAUGHAN
00695155 ....$24.95

BEST OF THE VENTURES
00695772 ....$19.95

THE WHO – 2ND ED.
00695561 ....$22.95

JOHNNY WINTER
00695951 ....$22.99

BEST OF ZZ TOP
00695738 ....$24.95

HAL•LEONARD® CORPORATION
7777 W. BLUEMOUND RD. P.O. BOX 13819
MILWAUKEE, WISCONSIN 53213

www.halleonard.com

COMPLETE DESCRIPTIONS AND SONGLISTS ONLINE!

Prices, contents and availability subject to change without notice.

0113